DEMO REELS & ARTHOUSE *MADNESS*

A COLLECTION OF DARK VERSE

Vince A. Liaguno

RAW DOG
SCREAMING
PRESS

Demo Reels and Arthouse Madness © 2025 by Vince A. Liaguno
Published by Raw Dog Screaming Press
Bowie, MD
First Edition

Cover art copyright 2025 by Scott Cole
Book Layout by Jennifer Barnes
Printed in the United States of America

All poems are original to this collection except:

"Chatroom Hustler" and "Tyro" first appeared in *Death in Common: Poems from Unlikely Victims*. Editor: Rich Ristow (Bandersnatch Books, 2010).

"Monday Shutdown" first appeared in *Help! Wanted: Tales of On-the-Job Terror*. Editor: Peter Giglio (Evil Jester Press, 2011).

"Shades of Madness in Paisley Patterns" first appeared in *Space and Time Magazine* (Issue #134, Fall 2019)

"Epoch, Rewound" first appeared in *Attack From the 80s*. Editor: Eugene Johnson (Raw Dog Screaming Press, 2021)

"Visiting Hours" first appeared in *HWA Poetry Showcase Volume VIII*. Editor: Stephanie M. Wytovich (Horror Writers Association, 2021)

"The Woods Are Dark" first appeared in *Shakespeare Unleashed*. Editor: James Aquilone (Crystal Lake Publishing, 2023)

ISBN: 978-1-947879-87-4
Library of Congress Control Number: 2024951697

RawDogScreaming.com

Advance Praise

"Like a seafaring Sigourney Weaver—which is one of a whole book of on-point references in here—Vince Liaguno sails out into the turbid, frothy waters of horror, and what he comes back with are these poems, which we can all feast on."
—Stephen Graham Jones, award-winning author of *I Was a Teenage Slasher*, *The Only Good Indians,* and the Indian Lake Trilogy

"Vince Liaguno's debut poetry collection transports the reader by way of dark poetic vignettes, each piece its own cinematic vision that are both familiar and chilling to the bone. Every line puts the reader on the edge of their seat as if they were watching each stanza unfold on some shadowy silver screen."
—Maxwell I. Gold, Bram Stoker Award® nominated author of *Tiny Oblivions and Mutual Self Destructions*

"Captivating madness runs like a film through Liaguno's mesmerizing collection. Every poem, another shadowy scene in the unwinding movie of this book. Each piece carried me from the first line, breathlessly to the final stanza. The delightful Afterword has a list of films, mostly horror, that inspired the dark beauty in his poetry."
—Linda D. Addison, multi-award-winning author and SFPA Grand Master of Fantastic Poetry

For Brian, whose love makes my life a poem.

Contents

"Film as dream, film as music. No art passes our conscience in the way film does, and goes directly to our feelings, deep down into the dark rooms of our souls."
—Ingmar Bergman

"We're all mad, the whole damned race. We're wrapped in illusions, delusions, confusions about the penetrability of partitions, we're all mad and in solitary confinement."
—William Golding, from *Darkness Visible*

"The hours wear on, while the surreal atmosphere of the asylum does not wear off."
—M.D. Elster, from *Four Kings*

Chatroom Hustler

1.

Raunchy sweet-nothings scroll
down the screen in rounded Arial fonts like
licentious love letters. Salacious innuendo –
His name is beeksteakcharlie62,
a Monmouthside daddy with condoms
in his wallet and a carrot top fetish.
I promise bareback carnal knowledge
for his spare change and a swig of Jim Beam.

I cruise the night, the nobody Johns passing,
their glance, glower, and hope
cast out like rainbow nets in the dark.
I spot him – virtual reality in the flesh – standing
expectantly on a tree-lined edge. I pass
the empty park benches between us.

I warily approach, awaiting Daddy's appraisal
of me, his would-be rentboy Romeo. Relief
spreads across his creased, weathered face
and his eyes take in my lanky sinew
and Opie innocence. In welcome, he passes me
a bottle of anesthetic party favors,
sleepy vapors that push me down, deep
into the white gauze of a Halloween memory,
my father wrapping me in thick mummy garb.

2.

I awake to face slapping.
"Cursive!" he shouts,
pointing at a sheaf of loose leaf,

coaxing my chronicles
I'm loath to recall:
neglected husbands
and vulnerable young fathers
and men of many cloths
I seduced by baits and lures.
My hand cramps at the end
of the page, my eyelids fall
like curtains drawing in on the night.
His hand grips my chin
and stuffs my own confession
into my mouth. I gag,
an auto-erotic asphyxiation
as my new Daddy nods his approval.
He smiles as his sharpened knife
cuts down to caress my throat.

Monday Shutdown

The mind slips as the nameless company drones surrounding me
click across keyboards in a staccato rhythm of terrifying efficiency.
Their faces are rendered featureless by too much artificial fluorescence,
corporate versions of children of the damned.

We sit centered between the razor-sharp outlines of cubicle cages,
tethered to the technology like one of Gacy's crawlspace boys.
Wires and cords and plugs wrap around our ankles like groping, grabbing zombie hands
trying to pull us down into communal graves dug by our own digits each day.

I'm color-blinded by all the black and white but mostly gray,
grateful for the occasional spray of red across the pavement down below our glass tower.
Another manic Monday rises from the beauty of the weekend
like a fire-spewing Godzilla looms over a shoebox-version of Tokyo.

I'm slowly being choked by the colorless, odorless air shooting through slatted vents,
the noxious remnants of the synthesized souls of a thousand terminated employees.
I can feel their presence everywhere, spectral spatters of the unemployed that
haunt and taunt and flaunt their disembodied potential all around me.

There is much to fear in this bland commercial land,
from the iron fist of the supervisor to the iron lung of the office itself.
Even paper shredders and thumbtacks have taken on an ominous countenance
in the wake of that unfortunate business with the garbage compactor and the intern.

Occupational hazards abound in surreptitious forms all around us.
From the dangers of toxic gossip to the terrors of office politics,
the slithering supervisors watch and wait for our fuck-ups and fumbles.
Like werewolves in tailored suits and Armani neckties, they hunger to pounce on their prey.

My officeland is but one strain of the corporate American disease,
an amalgamated outbreak of greed and ambition,

like bird flu and leprosy thrown into a blender and served over ice
in matching sterilized mugs emblazoned with the company logo.

So monstrous is this disease of mad mercantilism that hushed whispers
of "Don't drink the Kool-Aid" waft over and above the burping water cooler.
I've seen the aftereffects of Kool-Aid consumption;
the ugly transmogrification from automaton to robot wrangler.

Staple-sort-file, stack-collate-pile,
these are the monotonous rhythms and repetitions of our shift work sentences.
Shackled by this snarling business beast by the necessity of living,
my fellow droids and I survive to subsist on meager stipends doled out like crumbs to ravenous gulls.

Monday begins the cycle that never seems to end.
I'm drifting deeper, deeper into stupor from the strain of stress and the stress of strain.
I fear this land and its shuffling occupants, minds and hearts hollowed out and empty
like the pulpy insides of pumpkins at Halloween.

My head dips and there are introductions: chin meet chest, chest meet chin.
My eyes blink like lazy camera shutters, half-heartedly committing the images of officeland
to some floating piece of reluctant memory chip in the nether regions of my mind.
My eyelids flutter, then flicker out like the lights of a fog-enshrouded Antonio Bay.

I'm lost to the abyss of the Monday shutdown, spiraling into a stream of unconsciousness
where the horrors of officeland are muted and filtered through a heavy gauze
of self-preservation and delusion and fairytale clichés that evoke blissful hallucination.
Behind my mind's eye, I'm emancipated from this incorporated murder set piece.

Deep within my cerebral suppression, I'm Laurie Strode with a knitting needle;
I'm Alice with a machete to swing. I'm every final girl rolled into one,
with lung capacity to spare, lucky four-leaf clovers, and an arsenal of chainsaws
to castrate the faceless slasher of my officeland nightmares.

But like Laurie in the bedroom doorway and Alice in the canoe, the work week jumps up
for one more popcorn-in-the-air surprise. And like Nancy in her dream state,

my officeland Freddy finds his way into my daydream delusion,
with a glove full of cold conglomerate blades to cut out my heart and slash at my soul.

I'm a defeated dream warrior now, with veins sliced out of weary arms like strips of bacon
that my corporate master uses to jerk me around like a puppet on strings.
Even in the repose of the Monday shutdown, there is no escape from this cruel life sentence.
Through vacant eyes, I cling to the hope that it's five o'clock somewhere and pray for Tuesday.

Shades of Madness in Paisley Patterns

The affliction, one which resides in shades and variations of madness,
crawls amoeba-like across a dusty floor that meets a quartet of walls
adorned in fading Victorian wallpaper, paisley-patterned and perpendicular
in right angles, like crossroads outside an asylum of the mind.

Sanity tussles with encroaching darkness, gridlocked like a cerebral traffic jam,
all false starts and sudden stops that demand yield,
going nowhere except down the rabbit hole where mad hatters and lovelorn queens await
to host a tea party proper within *Le Théâtre du Grand-Guignol.*

Abstraction, crippling in its intensity, subjugates rationality behind vacant eyes
like a snake charmer enchanting wily serpents slithering up and out of woven baskets
made of wicker and wire and braided spines of rattan,
vindictive and venomous as their fangs puncture perspicuity with precision.

Senses and sensations dull amidst the madness—sight blinded, hearing deafened, touch numbed,
taste and olfactory rendered as mute as vocal chords severed
under the trilateral blade of a boxcutter slicing a throat in merciless caress,
its windpipe engorged with jugular potency and tendinous musculature.

Familiar faces hide behind caricatured masques within the insanity,
all madcap merrymakers lined up against dual sides of a great expanse of ballroom floor
approximating lifelike chess players on a checkered game board
embellished with twisted teardrops weeping for diminishing minutes.

The verse of madness rings not with lullaby but with warning,
like the ringing of the tide bell beneath the jetty in Aberdyfi Harbour,
a harbinger of rising seawaters and undulant currents that negates mythological deluge
with the certainty of bloated lungs after drowning.

Cranial infirmity gives rise to fig-shaped nightmares populated by conjured creatures,

frighteningly outlandish oddities summoned from the recesses of the subconscious
giving shape, pattern, and texture to these self-germinating incubuses
that writhe like perversions of Persian silk brocade.

Gray matter falls away in flecks like snow, gentle descent at odds with the violence of aftermath,
in which self slips lethargically out of view like the cruelest of eclipses viewed without filtration
until memories faded like Victorian wallpaper materialize in the unending dusk,
paisley-patterned and perpendicular to a mind's atrophied eye.

Frankenstein's Grammar

They arise, hungry.

An angry mob of armchair grammarians march on the castle
like torch-wielding villagers to set aflame syntactical abomination.
A grammatical monstrosity, misshapen and hooved,
has been gestating in a womb of words and twisted turns of phrase.

The compound and complex slumber amidst the cemetery claptrap
where linguistic logic and proportion have fallen sloppy dead among the corpses
of sentence fragments and mispronounced pronunciations.

Choleric contrarians bristle at misused alliterations and the corruption of grammatical conventions—
age-old and dutiful to the mother tongue, loyal like a companion dog—
and uttered in commoner's dialect distasteful to the sophisticate ear.

They disdain variation, deviation from normative etymological process,
constructing enclaves fortified by word harmony and sentence structure amidst the linguistic bedlam
breaching the parenthetical perimeter of their diagrammed complexities.

Gone are the days of adjectives tucked snuggly beneath subjective clauses
on ruler-straight diagonal lines, replaced with negligent lapses in syntax
that cause a twenty-six-member cast of letter blocks to tumble like an avalanche.

Slang and sloth run roughshod over pencil-perfect playbooks of rules and recipes
meant to keep civility on point, toppling well-spokenness into the darkest gutter of illiteracy
where the vermin feast on forensically precise paragraphs and passages.

But the scorned grammarians have risen up, from beneath piles of tomes building-high,
to reclaim order from the abject chaos. With mighty red scalpels, they dissect and diagram
with bloody abandon until this variant version of Frankenstein's monster is dead.

The castle still stands, roped off with yellow crime scene tape
that billows in the wind, a reposing reminder of the remnants of a viciously polite society
that rose up in defiance of language defiled.

They take leave, satiated.

Moon G(r)azing

I look 'round
and you've swallowed the moon,
flecks of moon dust tumbling down the back of your throat, scratching
like bits of hardened Swiss cheese.

Earlier, we gazed
through the long cylinder of the telescope,
hoping like kids on Christmas Eve to catch sight of miniature moon men, pogoing
like frantic sea monkeys at the bottom of a carnival goldfish bowl.

We wonder
why she grows bigger after we remove our eyes
from behind telescopic lens, her bulbous luminescence expanding, inflating
like a plastic pool raft left unattended on a compressor's hose.

We watch
with awe and terror as she continues to fill our field of vision,
craters becoming canyons, dimpled expanses of pale yellow, widening
like a kitchen sponge engorged and made voluminous with water.

We crouch
as she presses down, her nocturnal luster as brilliant as the daytime sun
and as hot as the circles within Dante's famed inferno, burning
like a red-tipped fireplace poker just home from the flame.

We inhale
to make room for her pasty pockmarked majesty as she presses forward still
commanding our rapt attention and squeezing us like lemons, insisting
that we make room because she's coming in.

We scream

as the she flattens our girth against stone, cold and coarse against our backs,
while our breath is taken in and held tight by razor-wire hems stitched strong, gasping
for air like displaced guppies spilled across synthetic shag carpet.

I breathe
sweet inhalations of respite from the moon's romanticized asphyxiation,
coming upon me as suddenly as nuclear holocaust on Hiroshima, wondering
how long you'll be able to harbor the moon and her merry men in your swollen gullet.

Honeymoon Suite

Four hundred silver tines clinking against crystal champagne flutes
reverberate in the reception's hazy afterglow, marking the midnight hour
as bride and groom cross the threshold in wedded bliss.

The honeymoon suite beckons, like an aged ambassador,
its tarnished wall sconces welcome with ambient, otherworldly light
that casts them in silhouette against faded, ornate wallpaper.

The newlyweds kiss, their tongues still sweet with the taste of strawberries
dipped in decadent chocolate and bitter with the tang of sharp cheeses.
An elixir of salty ocean air fuses with the mustiness of the chamber.

The beads and brocades of the young bride's wedding dress
whisper over threadbare carpet as she moves toward the bed,
bejeweled with dried rose petals and flanked by drooping wisteria.

The groom parts heavy curtains to proudly reveal an ocean view,
as his bride splays across the goose down comforter and lowers her head to the pillow.
Her eyes close as the sounds of undress mingle with her preconceptions.

The bride braces in anticipation of her groom as the mattress presses down.
She senses movement, too light, above and around and beside and underneath her,
as if the mattress gave way to air and she was floating on nothingness.

Her eyes open upon the translucent figure of a thousand different men,
myriad faces and features swirling in and out of focus like a fleet of schooners,
emerging and disappearing into the foggy night waters off the cruel Atlantic.

Her mouth opens to scream, her cry choked by misty tendrils probing mouth and throat,
as cold spectral digits slip the gold band from her ring finger,
the borrowed blue garter tightening like a tourniquet around her thigh.

Her body lifts and propels forward like a marionette without a master,
red-tipped toes dragging delicately behind her, conjugal bedgown billowing
like a failed parachute made of satin and lace.

Shards of glass confetti shower down around her
in celebration of her union with a thousand spectral men
as she passes from suite to veranda.

Like a bride carried over the threshold, she passes over the balcony rail
and slips from weightless arms,
hurtling toward the merciless rocks below.

Her ragdoll limbs writhe in a twisted parody of ecstasy
as gravity draws her down, muting her scream in the rush of wind
as she plummets toward the irreconcilable consummation of her marriage.

Tyro

I'm suspended, wrists bound,
while the parade of disconnected souls
passes by the writing table.
Their blood-soaked quills mark repeated ceremonies
without sequence,
the anarchy of an illogical Lechter now
as familiar as the scent of Thin Mint cookies.

I'm hanging, ravenous and parched,
as their penmanship becomes the meal du jour
and cursive strokes are eaten like crumbled cupcakes.
Like animated mannequins,
our guests jerk and pop and jolt and joggle
until stilled limbs litter the cellar floor in bedlam,
accidental puzzle pieces arranged in conscious disarray.

Death demands no discrimination
and corpses are afforded equal opportunity,
as the randomness of chance become fodder for curriculum vitae,
the screams of the ambitious, the interview.
Arrogance wears ingenuity like a ski mask,
snug and tight to the soul,
the subtleties of formula imperceptible
to the vacuity of society's order.

I'm dropping, wrists unbound,
my scribble and scrawl bleeding from numb fingers
onto a paper swan song.
Inkling and intimation fall surreptitiously
like taboo acts concealed between letters in a diary
hidden under the floorboards of an abandoned house.

Demo Reels & Arthouse Madness

Ingenuity wears doubt like a ski mask,
clinging hopefully to the conscience,
the intricacy of suggestion invisible
to the architect of casual depravity.

I'm sinking, remorse released,
into an opaque quagmire of contrition,
as apologies stream from cracked lips and
regrets seep from blood-rimmed eyes.
Fear of being lost among the abject randomness
rallies to restrain saliva that acts like acid
on the papier-mâché confession
of an architect's apprentice.

The catacomb darkens, life withers.
Wisps of waning hope escape me on dying breaths
as calloused fingers reach between my clenched teeth
and remove the epistle of revelations.

Deviance smiles as the sound of shredding paper,
like flesh ripping from bone,
follows me into the interminable night.

Dumbwaiter

1.

Pulleys up and pulleys down,
the young black boy hauls the plates and cups and bowls and silverware
to and from the grand dining room above.
The discarded remnants of meals told stories
like the ones his great-grandfather told about slave ships sailing toward a New World.
Useless fat trimmed by the privileged hands of white-gloved waiters
told of the well-mannered customs of debutantes and gentlemen
for whom gristle was the stuff of social distaste;
abandoned fowl bones bespoke the hunger and tenacity of officers and adventurers
for whom carcasses picked clean hinted at savagery beneath propriety.

2.

Pulleys up and pulleys down.
Always the same, except on the night of the day
the black boy's auntie made him sit on hard wooden pews
listening to tales of sin and punishment and echoes of the devil-made-him-do-it.
On the seventh night, the magic box went up empty and came down full,
and the remnants told a different tale,
one unlike any grown-up ever spoke or any storybook ever showed.
The bones were bigger, not of fowl nor goat nor boarbut picked haphazardly of
meat and gristle alike as if consumed by gentry
who had shrugged off decorum like a serpent sheds its skin.

3.

On seventh nights when daring shook him by the shoulders,
the black boy would hesitate before hoisting the empty pulley up,
leaning inside the magic box. The sounds of the Ambassador's quizzical guests
in conversation cannibalized by the slurping and cracking and snapping
of their raucous consumption drifted down the darkened chute, resembling nothing
of the polite murmurs of the proper folk who waltzed the grand lobby
and took up temporary residence in the rooms with stories on their walls.

Demo Reels & Arthouse Madness

Whatever the stories were, he was certain his seventh night stories were better.
And his came illustrated with bones.

4.
Pulleys up and pulleys down, the remnants were odd —
old Mrs. Tillinghaust's shoes, Mr. Bryer's specs, the constable's shiny badge.
Like reluctant castoffs, the orphaned belongings drifted down the dumbwaiter
wedged between garnish and gallbladder in crimson puddles on bone china.
Cook and dish washer got first dibs; they called it their seventh night booty
and praised Jesus and the saints. The rest went to the runners and busboys,
who praised the cooks and the dish washers for their false generosity.
But the young black boy who hauled and heaved got nothing
save for the calluses on his small hands.

5.
Pulleys up and pulleys down.
On a fifth day late in the sixth month, a new maître d'hôtel arrived.
The young black boy marveled at the man's pearly teeth – the whitest he had ever seen –
whose brilliance and shine were matched only by the emerald ring on his finger.
He was a cruel man, who barked and bit and demanded the lion's share
of the seventh-night booty. With whispers and sideways looks,
the cooks and pot washers lowered their heads and nodded reluctant assent.

6.
On that seventh night of that sixth month,
as unseen guests filed in above for their secret supper,
the young black boy handed the maître d'hôtel a platter
filled with succulent goose and turnips and corn bread.
The man balked and bellowed at the inverse delegation,
the cooks and pot washers, busboys and runners watching with fright and a little awe
as the young black boy told the man of the great seventh-night honor,
the privilege to serve the Ambassador's special guests.
The maître d grabbed the platter with a haughty humph and ascended to the dining room.

7.
Pulleys up and pulleys down,

the magic box brought great treasures to the kitchen that night.
Teeth, like great tusks from the hunted elephants of Africa,
lay decorated with parsley and lemon wedge in the center of the platter.
And, as the young black boy scraped grit and gristle and guts from the plates,
the cooks and busboys came to stand behind him.
He looked up, frightened of the consequences for having sent the maître d'hôtel
to such ghoulish end. But they just smiled and nodded and handed him an emerald ring.

8.
Pulleys up and pulleys down,
the maître d'hôtel with the pearly teeth visited the young black boy
in his dreams for six nights after that. He wore old Mrs. Tillinghaust's shoes
and Mr. Bryer's specs and the constable's shiny badge and spoke of the sins
of consumption and avarice and shouted commandments couched in fire and brimstone
and screamed for his teeth back and promised that God above had pulleys, too.
And when the little black boy awoke on the morning of the following seventh day,
he tugged his auntie's arm along toward the hard wooden pews, wanting–for the first time–
to hear the preacher's tales of sin and punishment and how the-devil-made-him-do-it.

Forum & Void

It resides, black and vacuous, with
the stench of rotting imbecility
among blackened hearts
pulsing with corrosive invective.
Green-eyed monsters spring
from crippled roses failing to bud
like flaccid organs in a desert drought
across barren acres of lapsed ingenuity.
Degeneration gathers like a toxic cloud
around smoky cauldrons spilling over
with vile ingredients of acid slander
and trifling annotations of inanity.
Stricken keys open portals into the vacuum,
luring the shuffling, egocentric zombies
into the virtual village of the damned where
parasites dwell like diseased vermin in an empty wine cellar.
Through the darkness, see the withered hands
grasping the feather-tipped quills so hard
that gnarled knuckles bleed spite onto
invisible paragraphs and pages.
Desperation and palpable revulsion reflect back
across the mirrored surface of faltering line

breaks, and failed sentences crumble into
high school musicals of pithy barbs.
Antipathy lies in opposition of feat
found decaying like rotten teeth,
punctuated by illuminated Arial pleas begging
to be plucked from suffocating obscurity.

Demo Reel

I.
Ominous piano notes signal autumnal bloodshed as
the jagged grins of butchered jack-o-lanterns
scream in the gruesome night of Samhain.

The actress is just nineteen and not first choice to babysit
but she's available and ready to scream her pedigreed heart out
like her mother once did scrubbing away her sins in the shower.

Hands deep in pockets of high-waisted and bell-bottomed jeans—
a snapshot of the quintessential innocence of a bygone era—
she arrives to bid welcome to the tricks and treats that will become her calling card.

II.
An old man weaves ghostly tales with the snap of his timepiece
as clippers slice through murky Pacific depths and
tendrils of creeping mist wrap vengeance upon leprosy of the hard-hearted.

Six must die, but she won't be one of them,
hitchhiking her way to church and a stranger's bed
as hands clotted with weeping sores shatter stained glass windows.

Her mother is back—fresh from the shower—to join in the screaming refrain
as the cleric dives deep in his cups to escape the inevitable encroach
of an angry sea captain back for what lies behind sacred stone walls.

III.
Scarlet drops spatter the celluloid images of prom kings and queens
as severed heads roll down the catwalk of adolescent retribution
for childhood games gone wrong amidst a conspiracy of silence.

Lockers slam as low-budget Canadians offer tax shelters and scripts
and the actress disco dances past death all the way to the bank,
skirting a ski-masked sibling with crank calls to make and an axe to grind.

Her pretend father rebukes the moniker of Shirley, her feigning boyfriend dies of AIDS,
in this heyday of horror, she is playacting among them, simulating screams
and working her way up to a royalty status she will rebuff in the afterglow.

IV.
Winter snow is soaked with crimson-like garish cherry snow cones
as chartered trains bullet along revenge-tinged tracks and passenger manifests
welcome Groucho and lizard men to the hellbound party.

She seems forever terror-bound now, screaming like a queen and scraping knees
in flight from the magician's assistant in drag with plastic cheekbones
who rattles the cage in his cadaver-flung fury.

Doc is a dick and Mitchy and Mo are dead and only Ben can save her now
with a convenient shovel that he uses to pummel and push,
escorting Kenny off the train for bad behavior like a ticket upgrade gone bad.

V.
Sun-drenched highways scorch in relentless sun
as Dingoes dodge murderous vehicular games
on macadam black and tarry with the stench of death.

She's still all thumbs, hitchhiking again across a land down under
trying not to scream this time even as the maniac motorcyclist
tightens the razor-sharp wire in black-gloved hands.

The slabs of meat are hung in the semi with care
in the hopes that career prospects soon would be there
amidst the protests of nationalists dismayed by stolen jobs.

VI.
The returning moon of All Hallows Eve surgically slices through Hippocratic oaths
and pastel scrubs run late as the skeleton crew gathers under the observant eye of Alves
to welcome their stretcher-strapped guest.

Loyalty brings her back but can't save her from the bad hair day

as she hops and hobbles away from brotherly malefactions
down the antiseptic corridors of a poorly-staffed third shift.

She proves a pro at homicidal evasion, sidestepping scalpels and bobbing butcher knives
as she limps toward the operating-room denouement of this closing chapter,
locked and loaded and driving off into the early-morning mist as the girl-group croons.

VII.
Twenty-score autumns after the first carnage of Samhain,
she realizes that undying evil thrives in pagan pop culture and demands revisit
of a career carved out like a cemetery grave with room to spare.

Older, she screams of wisdom and gratitude
while popping pills and swigging chardonnay from refilled glasses,
motherly instincts fueling her to avenge the horrors of 1978.

She's a homecoming queen even if she's avoided her hometown this time,
penning a loyalist love letter of cinematic nods and winks and recurring '57 Fords
while sharing last tender onscreen moments with her maternal secretary.

VIII.
Volts of electronic plasma bring slaughter to the denizens of salvage,
bio-mechanical incarnations of high-wattage death as she detours out to sea
to ferry a tugboat and chase aliens like a seafaring Sigourney Weaver.

She's wet and cranky and battered and bruised, chasing researching Russians
lost in the eye of a storm, but at least she gets an androgynous action figure this time,
even if it's all plastic stoicism and moveable parts.

This germ proves not to be contagious and she swears profanity and condemnation,
not afraid to bite this feeding hand nor to take remedy in the hope of chasing away
what she sees as an afflicting virus of mimicked mediocrity.

IX.
A penultimate bow as harvest moons burn bright orange in the glow of circles come full,
home once more to roost but flown over the cuckoo's nest in the blink of an eye,

falling…falling in irrevocable escape into a pile of raked leaves.

It seems hardly a fitting end—a double-dealing dupe—but it's hard to complain
when such royalty deigns to let them eat cake, scattering crumbs amongst the crows
and watching them scarf the nibbles up like hungry hordes as undead as the queen's brother.

This one's a chapter-closing cash grab, a means to a charitable end
and one (seemingly) last billet-doux to the Haddonfield diehards.
But—like tagline promises—evil can always be counted on to come home again…

X.
…and it does, this time with an indifferent eye toward the candy corns of our youth,
turning a blind eye to ancestry and cold-shouldering cinematic timelines
to (re)imaginatively reboot but not remake this second chance at a final encounter.

She's now a card-carrying AARP final girl, a grizzled and wizened gun-toting Annie Oakley,
lying in wait four decades for the man in the William Shatner mask
to come trick-or-treating one last time—or maybe three.

But this time she's ready in her homegrown labyrinth of sliding floors and booby traps,
her maternal protectiveness extending an extra generation. She's still the young girl staring
out the classroom window, only now she knows that this is—indeed—the bogeyman.

Visiting Hours

Alone
in an ever-shrinking box
with a porthole that teases
a freedom from droplet precautions
and the smell of disinfectant.

Isolated
amongst other elder tribesmen
who, too, have traveled long roads—
taken paths less chosen—
and now converge at this crossroads.

Sequestered
within pandemic pandemonium
where snippets of worry filter through the air
like the microscopic contagions
that seek entry through masked cavities.

Alienated—
cut off and set apart—
compartmentalized by sickness and syndrome,
in a suffocating casket
where space and time seem endless.

Disaffected
by social isolation
when the sliding glass doors
closed for the last and final time
and even that couldn't keep the monsters at bay.

Quarantined

as the virus stalks darkened corridors
that no longer ring out with shouts
of "Bingo!" or birthday song refrain
and even the ring of call bells has gone silent.

Reconciled
as the (wo)man in the puffy astronaut suit
announces that I finally have a visitor,
and I instinctively open my mouth in acquiescence
to at last receive my host.

Lost Traveler

Rainbirds sing
from atop a perch where madness roosts,
their melancholy warble a poem I could never write
even in the depths of my reticent thoughts
entombed within the airless sarcophagus of my mind.

Wings flutter
from tangles of branches arched in a parody of prayer,
the feathered flock rising from leafy camouflage
to take flight for points north made temporarily hospitable
by the changing ambience of a global thermostat left on.

Angry birds
pecking at my memories with gleeful abandon,
a hell-bound avian army hell-bent on picking my brain clean
like voracious zombies risen early from a nap,
their rotted stomachs growling with an appetite for recollections.

I'm waiting
in a dark, dark wood just outside the realm of conscious thought,
under occluded moonlight—a spectral remnant
dazed and displaced in the denouement of days
like a leftover ghost whose passport expired.

Fleeting thoughts
cram chaotically into a flimsy cerebral carry-on,
my last-ditch effort not to pay the extra baggage fees
that sanity airlines demands and tacks on to ticket prices
already far outside my budgetary constraints.

Days grow dark

in perpetual daylight savings, the nights longer, too,
stretching out before me like the black tarmac of a landing strip
with no lights and a pilot with no recall of how to land the plane
coming in sideways in the heavy crosswinds.

Flash forward—
and backward and in all directions with no direction,
I'm in the thick of the fog now like Mrs. Kobritz about to open the door
swatting miasma coils away from my face and pulling at
the muddle of spider webs stretching across my conscious mind.

I concede
to the parade of faces I should recognize with names I should know,
all with sad smiles now as they disregard my disjointedness
and lapses of rationality with the good-natured manners
of men who look away when a breeze catches a lady's skirt.

I'm writing
discombobulated poems about praying trees and crash landings
while images of seaman on sailing ships lost in the fog play on a looping reel
in perpetuity at the demented drive-in of my psyche. Suddenly, somewhere—
off in the distance—I hear the mad warble of the rainbirds singing.

Epoch, Rewound

A new wave of monster
creeps up from the well of time,
all Day-Glo colors as it slithers
out of an old bucket of Slime—
the kind with plastic worms—
and swallows everything in its path.

It springs upon the unsuspecting
like a worn VHS tape
ejecting from the pop-up mouth
of an antediluvian VCR,
only this beast with bad manners
isn't kind enough to rewind.

Its horrors trickle down
like Reaganomics,
as valley girls flee suburban malls—
their Bazooka wads
gagging them like spoons—
while goblins play synthesized soundtracks.

An ostentatious ogre
from an era of excess
bears down upon
flocks of seagulls in parachute pants
and gyrating Janes in leg warmers
and shimmering spandex.

It's backdated butchery,
like a night out at the drive-in
watching sorority sisters

getting strangled at slumber parties
and prom goers losing their heads
on catwalks of carnage.

Pandemonium ensues
as people shirk shoulder pads
and try to roller skate around the rink
beneath swirling disco balls
to evade this teething tetrapod
from the decade of decadence.

Clara's screaming for her beef,
while alien botanists in drag
demand a dime to call home
on makeshift landline telephones—
even though they can neither
speak nor spell.

The leviathan squashes
sixteen candles beneath its feet
while the club that meets for breakfast
narrowly escapes detention
and promises not to forget you
even as simpler minds prevail.

Even dragons hide in dungeons,
waiting for the beast to pass,
hoping it will return
to its temple of doom
before twisting everything in its wake
like a Rubik's Cube.

The world is filled
with echoes and reverberations
from the past,
a time when radio stars

were mercilessly struck down by video
and disco died in the street.

The monstrous 80's unleashed—
like alien eggs plopping out
of the queen's ovipositor
and seeping into pop culture consciousness
like acidic blood eating
through 8-track tape decks.

These are the facts of life now,
and few will be saved by the bell
even when your hair is jacked-up for Jesus
or Jheri-curled for Jackée—
it's a never-ending killer-thriller night
of creeps and demons and the dawning dead.

Ghosts of the Disco

I.

New York, 1982

Under great revolving mirrored balls, they danced.
Carefree and heavily influenced, the dancing queens
wore platform heels and shiny spandex that clung to their bodies
like passengers to the sides of lifeboats bobbing beside a ship
sinking into the murky waters of death.

No one seemed to fret that Donna had left her cake out in the rain,
paying more attention to weather girls who promised manly deluge
in these days of free love carried over and passed down by pot-smoking,
patchouli-scented hippies whose wood-stocked promises of peace
now pumped out of speakers at 120 beats per minute.

Bodies—slick with perspiration from poorly recycled air and the summer heat—
swayed and swirled in blithe unison, finding camaraderie in throbbing anthems
about getting checks and paying bills. These small-town boys were sycophants
to the rhythms around them as the shadowed DJ spun disco like spiders spin webs,
thick and sticky with the lust of a thousand men.

None of these boys saw the tall dark stranger step onto the dance floor that night
under strobe-lit cover until his shirt came off and then they lined up
outside bathroom stalls to collectively suckle on hardened nipples
and coax salty elixir from the monstrous thing that emerged from behind its
denim cage, angry and engorged with the fuming passion of repression.

Satiated desire begot stronger cravings, like the vampire to blood, and the dancing boys
danced harder and longer and with more men, belt notches keeping time
until sexual subjugations surpassed the urgent beat counts of the music
and the dancing men got lost in the uninhibited carnal abandon,
now slaves to the music and each other.

II.

New York, 1992

Under great revolving mirrored balls, they danced.
Slower now, with greater care and a wary eye cast out onto dance floors half full,
the dancing queens wore pastel shirts, collars upturned, alligators jutting out
over cotton stretched taut by pumped pecs. Nobody cared about Donna's cake anymore;
she sold out to the Christians peddling their own brand of pious pastry.

Bodies—slick with perspiration from night sweats and dotted with eggplant-colored lesions—
swayed and swirled in cautious accord, finding solidarity in wracking coughs
and virus loads, grasping at slippery hopes and tenuous advances. These small-town boys
were minions of the plague, recklessly abandoned to wasting syndromes
and doomed to indifference like pet shop dogs left to their own devices in a midnight fire.

Everyone knew the tall dark stranger now—and saw him in every pretty face that danced
past them, paranoia tempering libidos like elder porn. Kisses were furtive and sex tasted of latex,
the walks of shame longer and laced with post-coital terror and regret.
The mainstays were disappearing one-by-one like rabbits from a hat, entering the magician's
box but never coming out again.

The beauty of so many lovers is redacted to grief-quilted panels strewn out
in systematic rows across verdant lawns, stitched names and pittances of reminiscence
falling short despite the craftsmanship, failing to convey the inconceivable horror
of lives lost amidst apathetic shrugs and blind eyes that turned on dimes. Biblical comeuppance
to wash away the dirty gay is apparently divine intervention in some quarters after all.

Sometimes, as the first glimmers of dawn begin to cast away the enduring midnight
and the dancing fairies left remnant scurry to elude the light, the faintest hint of a four-on-the-floor beat
drifts out over empty New York City streets, a melancholy memento of long-ago dancehall days
and the ghosts of the disco who gyrate in perpetual ethereality, mournful in the dissonance of death,
and forever lamenting the fading taste of Donna's rain-soaked cake.

Awaiting You

I waited again for you today,
hoping that you'd show.
Hours passed—agonizingly slow—
as invisible hands gradually closed
the louvers on daylight
until I was left in abject darkness.

You must know I wait for you,
yet you hesitate to come.
Do you fear that I won't recognize you
in your current state?
I know you by heart—every strand of hair,
every molecule, every pulse of your vein.

No matter, I'll wait.
I've got everything and nothing
but interminable time wound tight
on a clock that ticks off hours
like minutes and minutes like hours.
Time, an odd and callous construct.

Yesterday—or maybe the day before—
a cardinal landed defiantly as I waited.
You're a funny one, I'll grant you that,
sending this red-feathered reminder
that you've yet to show.
Rub it in, I'll wait.

Waiting now so long,
I've somehow lost track of the seasons,
forgetting their familiar sequence.

One minute I'm planting mums, then marigolds,
the next I'm lamenting that I've left
my gloves in the car.

This can't be it—a slab of stone
amongst systematic rows
and endless waiting
in this wasteland of the dead
that's like an airport full of departures
but no incoming planes.

I'm standing there, alone, at the gate
staring at an arrival board
that never seems to update.
In this empty waiting area,
the seats are as solid as frozen earth,
but even in cold, my warmth awaits.

I'm waiting for you to disembark
from this terrible journey you've taken.
You must be tired—I know I am.
Traveling can be so tiresome.
I still remember the day you left,
packing light and late for your flight.

I snap alert at every movement,
every shifting shadow,
from the edge of the tree-lined border
encircling this depressing depository,
thinking it's you, but knowing it's not.
Still, I await you. Please, draw near.

Other

Fear the otherness, the nebulous monstrosity of unknown
as it treads along hardened soils in gardens of odium
cultivated with rows of hate-seeds deeply sown.

With tinted skin, it's an unidentified foreign object
that walks amongst us in this war of the worlds
spinning out of control on a saucer-shaped axis.

With an exotic tongue from planets afar, sounds emanate—
linguistic jibber jabber that reinforces the extraterritorial
eccentricity of this stranger abroad and out of context.

The other is never far from out of focus,
an alien eyesore that assaults senses by sheer virtue of being
and loathed without logic beyond its state of dissimilarity.

Take cover underneath sturdy white cotton hoods, camouflaged by night,
to embrace in the shadows what the day must not discern
for the scorn is quite ugly in the noontime's glow.

Like a good villager, grab pitchfork and torch and give pursuit,
chasing the other back to its native habitat,
cornering it at the intersection of Catch and Twenty-two.

Prick the other with sharpened prongs and the bombshell
will burst from the box of enlightenment like a spring-loaded clown,
bobbing and bouncing in the disgraceful truth of a manufactured war.

The other, it bleeds,
hemorrhages the same blood as those from the village,
shares the same distant DNA of others past.

The other is them.
The other is us.

Sense of Nothing

Nothing is a blank canvas,
barren of color and shape
a featureless landscape of insignificance
stretched taut to infinity.

Nothing is silence,
an absence of sound
deafening in its muted white noise
that burrows like an ear worm.

Nothing is flavorless,
a palate rendered pointless
and made dull of discernible tang or spice
sliding down the gullet into an abyss.

Nothing is without texture,
an imperceptible surface wiped clean
with an intangibility that can't be touched
by hand or smacked with affectionate lips.

Nothing is an unscented void,
an odorless plume of emptiness
that's as nondescript as oblivion
and as ambiguous as a rhetorical question.

In this cryptogram of sensory deprivation,
everything, everywhere, all at once is naught.

Carnivàle

1.
'Round and 'round it goes
the click-clack-clack-click of the striking spokes bombinating
like typists keying in manic rhythm,
the barker behind the booth bellows
and bestows his best gimcrack and gewgaw
– much foofaraw over the randomness of numerical chance.

2.
Across the midway, the fat lady sits atop the funhouse
having ingested a cavalcade of candy apples and cotton candy and corn dogs,
fried dough and funnel cakes and kernels of popped corn
that threatens to spill forth from her ample plastic bosom
which peels and flakes in the hot Jupiter sun.

3.
She straddles her house of frolic in perpetuity, eyes fixed across the fairgrounds
for signs of Goldie and Meryl and their magic cans of spray paint
that will shellac her back to her former zaftig glory.
Inside the belly of this beast are mirrors that elongate and crunch,
stairs that wiggle and waggle, strobing lights that remind you of a mushroom high
– all trippy bliss.

4.
But you know what Tobe did to poor Amy and Cooper, Richie and Liz,
so you make for the banquet of bumper cars that glide and crash
into one another like drunken salamanders in the Yemen,
hoping that Madame Zena's fortune-telling is less prophecy
and more sideshow act and that chawbacon Gunther keeps the mask
on his Frankenstein monster.

5.

Duck under a tent flap for the all-American horror of the freak show
where alligator men terrorize bearded ladies knocking bottled babies off the shelf,
where the hermaphrodite mermaid and human pincushion
dazzle and disgust in their anatomical oddity – like Bowie covered by Elsa Mars,
crooning, cawing in the spotlight of a thousand vultures
in equal abomination of night and nature.

6.

The puppet theater beckons, bidding whimsical welcome
as the ventriloquist sits center stage, bookended by dancing marionettes
jerked and jiggled by invisible hands somewhere out of sight.
Sound seemingly emits from the moving mouth of the dummy-star whose plastic eyes
joggle back and forth as if besieged by puppet seizure,
who seems mighty comfortable considering the size of the puppetmaster's fist.

7.

Show over, you fork over three tickets to the pimpled ride attendant
for a spin on the Ferris wheel that sends you up and around, around and down,
with momentary apex views that give glimpse to the scurrying carnival-goers below.
Like Asian extras fleeing Godzilla, they dash from tent to tent, from ride to ride,
adrenaline junkies for the kind of small-town macabre that only a traveling sideshow
could bring, one both erected and dismantled in a fortnight's time.

8.

At midnight sharp, the carousel horses slow, the scratchy carnival music grinds to a stop,
the two-headed calf retires for the night, and Madame Zena throws a silk scarf over her crystal ball
while the keepers of the carnivàle escort the last of their nightly guests out through the gates.
As the lights shutter across the midway in melancholic succession,
only the funhouse fat lady remains focused on the distance beyond.
It's always the first night and the last night in this temporary land of mad fun.

Desert Succulent

It basks in the blazing noonday sun,
a picture of botanical innocence—green, swollen leaf-flesh
gathered and held sturdy by strong stem
against an arid landscape as cruel and unforgiving as a scorned dominatrix.

Beneath its waxy cuticle, thick, gooey mucilage coagulates like a botanic blob
ready to trap its prey like the sticky-paper roller ensnares vagrant lint
while its Crassulacean acid metabolism stalks mist and moisture
under the cloak of night—like a vegetal vampire.

Reptiles—scaly, slithering, and sanguine in their mission—avoid the succulent
like altar boys are taught to sidestep the post-Mass sanctuary
knowing that not all monsters announce their malevolence
by wearing tell-tale masks.

Subsistence itself is an eerie irony in this waterless wasteland,
a shadeless Sahara where sunbaked sand is punctuated
by jagged rocks jutting up like impotent pillars
without stature or purpose or function.

While everything around it dehydrates, withers, and dies,
the succulent remains plump, engorged with liquid lifeforce,
evidence of nocturnal mischiefs when the vastness of the azure horizon
cedes to the shadowed stretch of nighttime camouflage.

Only the nightcrawlers—the unfortunate centipedes and millipedes—
that hastily creep past the far wiser tarantula to unluckily
seek shelter beneath that swollen leaf-flesh discover the truth
behind the folklore whispered amongst the plant-folk.

The succulent is silent in its desiccation,

more a casual absorption than a big gulp, nondescript in its botanic brutality
but no less consequential to the many-legged critters
that unwisely seek asylum from the spider beneath the mask.

The botanical incubus of the desert lies in wait,
its patience as eternal as the parched flatland in which it reposes.
The accursed triffids may have had their day,
but the night belongs to the enduring desert succulent.

Cinderella Boy

Cinderella boy, once golden and fair-skinned,
wanders the city streets, lost in the rubble of time
amidst an abyss of soulless bodies
and panhandling brokers of the flesh.

He lives in self-imposed disqualification,
a recalcitrant bottom roaming amongst
the hungry ghosts of hopelessness
like a frustrated showgirl relegated to the back chorus row.

Cinderella boy has no glass slippers to lose,
his feet swollen with the edema of poor choices,
each curb and uneven sidewalk square a chore like
navigating a drunken dance.

Dreams of grand stardom once drove him
before necessity threw him to the famished
who demanded a pound of flesh for a pittance
after which he was discarded harshly.

Cinderella boy wore the grandest ballgown once,
one that billowed in imaginary breezes
and swung out wide when he twirled
into the back of his father's closed fist.

Face scraped raw against the concrete sidewalk,
Cinderella boy ran down the block away from purgatory
and straight into hell, where devils of all shapes and sizes
were only too eager to rip off his pretty dress.

No pumpkin carriages or handsome princes

will come calling for Cinderella boy—
but there was that priest with a foot fetish once
who fed him butternut squash soup.

Father John had a kindly post-coital face,
and a soothing voice once his own appetites
were satiated, but even he, too, suffered
compassion fatigue once the bowl was empty.

Cinderella boy allowed himself to be led
down to the church basement where those like the cleric
were also eager for carnal communion,
and he lay reverently prostrate as one about to receive.

Held down against cold pavement, he lost track
of how many sets of hands poked and prodded him,
but he didn't cry because the sins of a hundred men
were still more comforting than the single fist of a father.

Random Selection

Begging the question why,
whose answer never satiates
as if understanding it somehow
brings relief from the weight
of embedded images
outlined in white chalk
on sidewalk cement
like a game of hopscotch
gone unspeakably wrong.

Motive by conjecture
awash in a sea of possibilities
as vast as oceans combined,
feebly undertaking to assign
an order and logic
to the chaos of carnage
that in due course
will reduce pretext
to mere odds and probabilities.

No—it wasn't the impromptu
stop at the corner bodega
for the bottle of red
whose oaky bouquet mixes
with the metallic-sweet smell
of the blood, its robust tannins
and sandalwood accents
now congealing and mingling with
it in curbside coagulation.

No—it wasn't the choice of clothes,

the ripped jeans and wrinkled tee
making no discernible difference
in who or when or where
or how brutal or how many times
the knife blade punctured skin
before sliding out, bloodied
but firm in its resolve
to repeat, replicate, duplicate.

No—it wasn't political rhetoric
or a photo posted to Instagram,
neither voyeuristic audition
nor pre-meditated selection
based on carbon footprint
or the color of a car or a
telltale tattoo glimpsed
in the anonymity of virtual
adult playgrounds.

Every Sophie makes her choice,
and there is no turning back
once the invisible mark of happenstance
is made for the angel of death
to zero in on its prey—oblivious
and haplessly unaware—lost
in the mundanity of everyday
life and loves and too many texts
that distract from the road ahead.

Don't be afraid
of what's under the bed;
it's the generic passerby
who can kill you at random,
without warning or foundation
or any small degree of mercy
or consideration of dinner

on the table or kids waiting up
or a puppy expecting to pee.

Swift, cold-blooded,
without calculation
beyond the rush-release,
a chance encounter
on a city street
brings with it cheerless certainty
that what was anticipated
was just a wrong turn
down a dead-end street.

Discomfort Food

I awake to the gray
like every other day of late
tangled in the sheets
of my complicated bereavement.

I will my feet
to slip over the edge of the bed
and burrow within the soft tufts
of deliberately set moccasins.

I amble out of the room,
down the hall, down the stairs
with no real confidence
that anything different awaits below.

The smell of fresh-brewed coffee—
once an olfactory cheerleader—
burns my nose in its cloying insistence
upon weekday normalcy.

The ill-mannered Mr. Coffee is but a symptom
of this suffocating household compassion,
where toast and marmalade and
fresh-baked scones converge

in their half-baked effort to revive
my depressed spirit
with their aromatic empathy
and savory sympathies.

As I draw nearer the kitchen,
my melancholy wills me to pivot—

to instead turn left, walk toward the front door
and out into the stark white of winter beyond.

Outside, there is only vast emptiness
as far as the eye can see,
my emotional whiteout reflected back
on the featureless horizon.

It's cold, frigidly so.
With each step outward into nothingness,
I put distance between myself and
the benevolent Mr. Coffee and his menu companions.

Gastronomic aromas, once comforting, dissipate
into sensory deprivation
as snow slips over the tops of my moccasins
and chills my forward-moving feet.

Steps become feet become miles
as I put distance between unwanted mollification
and my destination ahead—
a journey into an oblivion

where grief can suffocate a soul
into submission, where sorrow can flourish
unabated without the shackles of condolence
or the crushing weight of kindness.

One more step—and an audible crack punctuates
the poverty of my senses.
I am descending another staircase, this one without steps
or railings or landings below.

As my body drifts downward,
the comforting numbness creeps up and within.
Waterlogged moccasins finally anchor me
to the bottomless depths of my lamentation.

The Night He Came Out

On Halloween night, 1983,
the young boy took a butcher knife
to his mother's wedding dress.
He plunged it in, without mercy
or concern for its well-being,
savage in his purpose.
He hated everything the dress
had once embodied—but loved the
beaded bodice and filigree—
so matrimonial massacre seemed
the logical path for him to take.

He used the shredded wedding gown
to fashion quite the dress—
marrying its bead-trimmed bodice
to a pair of stretchy dark hose
under a cloud of poufy tulle.
Lacey white gloves and neon-pink pumps
and dangling crucifix earrings
completed his look.
As he'd adjusted his blond wig
in the mirror that night,
a shape in the shadows watched.

Fists clenched in disapproval,
the shadow-shape leapt out
of the slatted closet doors
to stab at the air with pointed slurs
and rebuke the boy's evil within.
The boy in the dress filled his lungs
and screamed, knowing

that there was nowhere to hide
now that the closet doors were open.
He ran from the man
in the William Shatner mask
and never looked back.

When he stumbled out
onto suburban streets,
the boy was transformed.
Innocence lost under autumnal canopies
of fiery reds, oranges, and yellows,
he regrouped, smoothing his
tulle skirt and adjusting his wig.
The boy straightened and strutted,
a would-be early-era drag Madonna
on the hunt for tricks and treats.
He would survive—a final girl for the ages.

Drowning Delilah

In my mind's eye, I see Delilah die.
The panic in her eyes as she came up after going under,
her arms flailing as rolling waves lifted and lowered her,
bringing her closer to shore but then out again in cruel tease and torment.

In her mind's eye, I stood on the shore.
The panic in my eyes as she came up after going under,
my arms flailing as she was lifted and lowered on rolling waves,
as if I could gesture and gesticulate her to safety.

In my mind's eye, I see Delilah drown.
The knowledge of my cowardice in her eyes as she went under for the last time,
her arms straight up in an inverted dive,
streamlining her descent to the murky depths of certain death.

In my mind's eye, I see Delilah reposing in the night ocean.
Her hair swaying lazily above her in the deep-sea current,
her arms half-heartedly extended before her,
forever outstretched like a waterlogged sleepwalker.

In my mind's eye, I see Delilah's toes curl into the sand on the ocean floor,
taking tentative steps forward in her new gravity-reality,
her motions fluid and undulating with the tide,
as if swaying to a gentle musical composition only she can hear.

In my mind's eye, I see Delilah rise from the sea,
emerging from the seafoam with seaweed draped
like Spanish moss hanging from the branches of bald Cypress trees,
a macabre parody of swampland ecology.

In my mind's eye, I know that Delilah has come for me.

I can hear the water squish-squelch out of her sponge-like skin
as she ambles toward me, arms open in embrace,
an escort into the rolling waves and shadowy depths to her new home.

In my mind's eye, I see myself die.
There is no panic in my eyes as I come up after going under,
and I am still as I'm lifted and lowered on the rolling waves—
a current of conscience washes over me and dissolves my guilt in the vast night ocean.

Storytelling

Who doesn't love a good story?
Tales from tomes and standalone concoctions
of words and phrases twisted to convey
morals and lessons and happy endings
where the boy gets the girl and the everafters
are fixed and firm and rooted in forever.

But the best stories are the ones served on ice.
Yarns so shocking they send shivers up spines
mired in the crackles of crepitus,
tether minds to an endless phantasmagoria
where reality and illusion meld
like burning skin to polyester-blend sweater sleeves.

The best storytellers know how to serve up dread.
Not the ones who projectile vomit folklore
or the ones who can paraphrase Grimm—no,
the best tellers of tales boldly embellish
and paint word pictures with garish colors
in dramatic shades of Giallo.

Did you hear the one about the turtle-killing lesbians?
Or the ghosts of the nursing home who fling shit
and bang bed pans and lace the mashed potatoes
with laxatives and crushed-up erection pills?
How about the little ditty about Jack and Diane
and their killing spree through seven convents across six states?

Who gives a shit about harsh seacoast winters?
Stories so bland that they neutralize stomach acid
like Tums after an all-you-can-eat food orgy

at the buffet of mediocrity and cerebral safety,
anecdotes that elicit yawns of complacency amidst
the atrophying minds of listeners.

Nothing more egregious than a blasé storytime, kids.
Wasted words strewn halfheartedly together
with neither the flair of flamboyance nor
the élan of exaggeration, literary duds that land
flat like a skipping stone and cause barely a ripple
on the surface of the imagination.

Fuck *once upon a time* and *happily ever after*, all those
lazy literary conceits that lull into false senses of security.
Good storytellers are like doomsday preppers
who spin conspiracies of fear wrapped in quaint fable jackets,
who know the fictions that demand attention are the ones
with the piranhas' serrated bite.

Did you hear the one about the rap star
who fell from the wing of a plane?
Or the sad tale of the baby trapped under the tree?
Yeah, the good stories are like six-car pileups,
the ones you see from the backseat window as the chaos crawls by
with cadavers and kidneys shaken loose on the shoulder.

Give me disturbia and Dahmer details over Disney any day,
tales of tarpaulins and toe tags and madness in the morgue
or the legend of storytellers who become wolves at the end.
Enrapture their frightened little minds with macabre machinations
that leave them wide-eyed and pants pissed,
eager for the next bedtime tale of terror—such bliss.

Missing Adults

New York TYG 7542

Silver Hyundai sedan, last seen leaving a 7-11 lot.
Driver is a red-haired junkie so those tuning in to the eleven o'clock news
have already made up their minds: she's not missing, she's high
on crack or meth, probably selling her body for a hit.

Pennsylvania GPN 8611

Black Ford F-150, last seen at the turnpike toll.
Driver is a blue-collar warehouse worker who smokes too much
and saves too little, an all-American working-class Joe,
as average and nondescript as the tribal tattoo circling his left bicep.

Indiana 874 CEF

Navy blue Honda Civic, last seen leaving the hometown game.
Driver is a high-school kid, his face full of acne and head filled
with dreams of post-Hoosier life, with watching cornfields recede
in the red glow of taillights through a smudged rearview mirror.

Kansas 936 JENN

White Volvo, last seen in the grocery store lot off K-232.
Driver is a church-going mother of four who wears sensible shoes
and swears when no one's around, her breasts firm despite hungry
children and the effort it takes to keep up appearances.

Colorado 088 VEP

Red Nissan XTerra, last seen leaving Beaver Creek, skis strapped to the roof.
Driver is a downhill skier always in search of the next snow-packed
adrenaline rush and double black diamond: he's as freestyle in the bedroom
as he is on the slopes, an equal opportunist Casanova.

Nevada 114 LMS

Cream-colored Mercedes-Benz, last seen pulling out of the Paris underground.
Driver is a trans escort exceptional at her craft, keeping both her schedule
and her tummy tight for the out-of-towners, mainly businessmen
who like a little cherry twist on their happy ending sundae.

California 7HMJ009

Red Camaro convertible, last seen parked outside the Last Call.
Driver is a silver-haired fox who enjoys '80's hits and hot boys
with Daddy issues: he's a generous blue-eyed Sugar Pop with candy to spare
and a Bow Wow Wow CD in heavy rotation.

Oregon 895 DPY

Standard-issue box truck, commercial plates, last seen heading toward Cullaby Lake.
Driver is a quiet man—sullen some would say—a cross-country collector
of spare parts for his special art, a red-haired mannequin adorned
with tribal tattoos and flesh-colored postcards from points on a map.

Abandoned cars and discarded limbs litter the countryside he's crossed,
all those misplaced people who missed connections, faces stapled side-by-side
on cork where countless sets of eyes miss a connection of their own,
just missing adults reduced to the sum of their disposable parts.

American Psychos

I.
Pressure builds,
like steam under the lid
of a covered copper pot.
It expands and stretches
like an over-inflated tire
pumped too full of air
and threatens to detonate
like baby spiders from their
wolf-mother's egg sac.

In the cavity of madness,
bedlam bubbles up
like battery acid boiling
over the top of papier-mâché
volcanos stuffed with bile
and bilge water and forbidden
fantasies that cloud judgments
like malignant mists cover
grocery store windows.

Rage seeps
into receptive veins
though an intravenous drip
of toxic masculinity
like radioactive contagion,
pulsing with misogyny
and hatred of everyone
constricting blood flow
to a coagulating heart.

Black soul beneath blacker eyes,

conscience is gutted
by ravenous parasites
who leave scant trace
of the little boy
who played with dead things
in his treehouse of horrors.
Body grows, mind warps
and humanity arrests.

II.
Bateman pontificates
on how hip it is to be square
before introducing Mr. Allen
to the chrome axe blade
that bests his business cards,
while Jack builds his house
in between offering rides to Uma
and creating dioramas
with frozen friends.

Beauty is a crime
punishable by death,
or at least that's what Zito says
as he pays oedipal homage
to his maternal mannequins
before flipping his custom-made
wig of many colors
as hallucinated hookers and whores
tear him to shreds.

Daryll Lee has a pen pal
long after Hudson is hung
and left locked and housebound
in hi-tech isolation
before a copycat comes calling
with his ordered list

and meticulous set pieces
to coax the good doctor
to peer out through her looking glass.

Mr. Brooks is all thumbs
as he takes twelve steps
to rid himself of an inconvenient alter ego
and a protégé with Polaroids.
Seven deadly sins
were John Doe's murderous motif,
while Norman's shtick
was creating a motel hell
with luxuriantly warm showers.

Ripley does a killer impersonation,
while Ryder takes his act on the road.
Casanova kisses all the girls,
Kramer likes puzzles and games.
Henry and Otis work in tandem for a while,
but Angelina's guy collects bones solo.
Serial killers all, but no two alike
since not all psychoses are created equal.

III.
Cinema and psycho,
a fine-tuned formula
of violence and charisma—
time-honored and as popular
as warm apple pie on Thanksgiving.
Spectators watch wide-eyed
as cat stalks mouse
in a slow tango of death
that ends when the music stops.

Reflected ripples
of societal miscarriage and

the perverted privilege
of man's entitlement
to dominate and subjugate
viewed through the
mirrored lens of arrogance
and misshapen mediocrity
masquerading as superiority.

Film reflects
the damaged mind
of the scorned psychopath—
but where do the vulturine
predilections of Sam
and Jeffrey and John
receive *their* nutrients?
Embedded behavior—
or too many smothering hugs?

Such musings
are but rainy-day speculations
for the analyst to woolgather—
to turn and twist in minds
hard-wired for such insights
into broken teacups
whose sharp shards
rip and shred the flesh of feet
that traverse crossed paths.

Ripcord Failure

Falling dreams
dog me since my earliest recollections,
vivid as petrichor on a late August day
or the taste of tomato soup and grilled cheese
after playing in backyard snow mountains.

Tumbling thoughts
chase me down from pillow heights,
the gravitational pull stronger than the heaviest
goose-down blanket tucked under the mattress
tighter than a drag queen's cock.

Descending daydreams
trip me up in narcoleptic surprise,
pinning me to the office chair and erasing
my agenda of tasks and chores and errands
from the vertical lines of my daily planner.

They drop downward
from castles in the sky filled with kings
and queens with miles of silken blond tresses
that cascade over the citadel walls
like a golden vanilla wafer waterfall.

All those plummeting pipers and pipedreams,
fastening seatbelts in the first-class accommodations
on flights of fancy destined for crash landing
in fields of dreams already strewn with the
wreckage of misplaced realities.

I'm plunging headfirst
into delusions with no parachute—
a freefall into the oblivion of madness—
hands instinctively reaching, fumbling, grabbing, grasping,
pulling imaginary ripcords in the air.

Arthouse Asylum

In a basement,
water drips in poetic ruminations
that tell dozens of tales and show
horrific visions of tormented demons
and pastoral country landscapes
in parallel and interwoven ways—
reduced to blighted post-nuclear badlands
that resemble an eclectic jazz mural
shot in minimalist black and white.

In the asylum of the arthouse,
one must abstract to transcend,
deviating and dovetailing
from the surreal to the existential,
suffocating on allegory and
relinquishing an outlaw psyche
to the unanticipated consequences
of aliens trolling Glasgow roadways for sex
and stripping tricks of their humanity.

In the gulf between celluloid frames,
the clarity of realism is violated
like rules in a rubric discarded
in the name of artistic ambiguity
and the linear conduits
through which narratives flow
are purposefully contorted
into intersectional intercuts,
aesthetic allusions.

In tunnels beneath this madhouse,
runs an underground railroad
of experimental deviancy,

avant-garde terrors like
the inhumane circus performer
who believes that he is Jesus Christ
with a stigmata that bleeds pus
and a crown of gaily-striped birthday candles
that offer electroconvulsive benefits.

Within the bedlam,
Warhol and Lynch stand keen
with expressionistic electrodes,
ready to explore themes
of identity and disconnection,
to counter the unbendable symmetry
of convention's concrete jungle
long before the deconstruction
of Dylan or Harry.

Lost in the labyrinth—somewhere—
in uncharted depths of symbolism,
what you see isn't
what you're meant to see
but what you should see
if only your insight
was as sharp as the projector
emanating images into constructs
far beyond the canvas screen.

Misery Is Not a Book

Grim voyeurs
look through windows
at weightless souls whose
hearts of glass shatter
into untold fragments
of lives unlived.

Suicide seekers
forage through forests in Japan,
wading through a sea of trees
and treacherous roots
in search of absolution
and self-inflicted exodus.

Horizons like roads—
long, winding, black and barren,
less traveled and not taken—
are empty, vast, and desolate
stretches of mindless beauty
like infinite space.

Madness—like an antidote
to a noxious world
mired in disharmony
and cognitive dissonance—
provides an escapeless room
in which to burrow.

Gloominess suffuses essence,
haunted by the ghosts
of sidestepped interventions

and noble purposes
that cast them deeper
into abject aloneness.

Displaced and vagrant
in a house where
ambiguity and indifference
dwell in guarded pots
that never seem to boil,
they succumb to darkened fate.

Pain is totality, reality,
entirety and actuality,
a tsunami muscle
that pries open the soul
and smothers potency
with snuff-film precision.

Misery is not a book
of flimsy pages
that turn on whim—
she's a goddess of grief
with a vice-clamp clutch
that crushes the core.

There is no rebuke
and little reprieve
once her fangs of fatalism
puncture epidermis
and begin to siphon off
the rivers of lifeblood beneath.

Misery leaves a shell
in her wake—a hollowed-out
tusk of lost promise
that shrivels like a discarded
snakeskin and falls to pieces
under the weight of breath.

Summer Camp, Parts I and II

I.

I first went to summer camp when I was 12, eager to come of age having just gone trick-or-treating and met my one and only schoolboy crush with the androgynous first name. The campfire song was corny and the camp counselors horny, making google eyes at each other and then sneaking away to do adult things. Their employment didn't last long, but they certainly got their severance. The cook came to town, backpack slung, with a bad sense of direction. We immediately hit it off—she was an animal lover. Dogs and goats, but don't call them kids. Enis touched her ass but she never did seem to mind, and I was sad when she came up short after that second hitch that left everyone else wondering what was for dinner. Hairy Steve owned the camp but, boy, was it a mess. Townies said he was crazy to re-open with so many ripped archery targets and missing gutters and all that blood soaking the campgrounds. He was pretty creepy, too, as Alice perched on that ladder with care in hopes that the other camp counselors soon would be there, but Sandy will tell you he was a mighty good tipper. The pick-up truck arrived on a wave of twanging banjoes and brought three more in. Brenda and Bill emerged from the woods to welcome, while Steve ran to town before the big storm rolled on in. While the cat was away, the nubile mice decided to play, hitting the lake for a swim—the sight of Jack's Speedo-encased slab of bacon searing into mind and memory—and some faux resuscitation before a misplaced snake met the end of Bill's machete. Crazy Ralph showed up, bringing his messenger of God who spoiled dinner with prophecies of doomed unity, and then it was a visit from motorcycle cop guy who I don't remember much because I was distracted by Ned's tighty-whities. Marcie and Jack canoodled lakeside a bit while Neddy sulked off in search of a good throat lashing, but before Marcie could finish her tale of raining pebbles and rivers of blood, a storm tore over the valley like a son of a gun. With Ned taking top bunk, Jack and Marcie made love before Marcie took a pee break and poor Jack got skewered from below before he could even catch a high. Rain-slickered Marcie, amused by potty poetry, does a bad Hepburn imitation before catching the shadowed axe—but at least she died with minty-fresh breath. A randy game of strip monopoly raged back at the main cabin, with Bill losing boots at Baltic and Brenda counting the minutes until he arrived at the gates of her Kentucky home, until windblown finances brought the real estate deals to an end. Brenda heard a cry and went to take a look, while Bill strummed the guitar and Alice stoked the flames with a twig. Brenda's earlier archery task foretold her off-camera end, as did Bill's previous trip to the generator shed. Poor Alice was left to find them all—Annie propped in the passenger seat, Bill pinned to the door— then relief washed over her as headlights flooded the floor. A little too convenient that lady in the blue turtleneck was, with motherly hugs and shrugs of dismissal as Alice pled about this one and that one—each of them dead. *Did Alice know about Jason, the boy who had drowned?* Shoddy supervision and lackluster swimming skills apparently do not make a good match. A protracted chase and a moonlit beachside brawl saw blue turtleneck lady lose her head in anger, shaking her bloody fist right to the very end. Alice is tired and fucked in the head, so she sets sail in a canoe to catch some Z's. The law arrives to a picturesque scene as a melancholy melody wakes Alice from her post-massacre slumber to join the boy with the misshapen head for a surprise early morning swim. Alice awakes, screaming in sweat, surrounded by sanitized white as the cop confirms, yes, they're all dead. But the body count is short one, as Alice, sweet Alice, learns as she stares forlornly into her memories of summer camp…now my memories, too.

II.

I returned to summer camp thirty-eight years later on an auctioned whim, eager to launch the next half a century and still faithfully monogamous to the same androgynously-named schoolboy crush who would once again go trick-or-treating later that year. This time the camping was a three-dimensional encounter, surreal as I traversed the same rutted road that Ned's red pick-up once bounced down with substandard shocks. The presence of the camp counseling ghosts from '80 haunted every nook and cranny of the musty cabins still standing erect in defiance of time. Even the lit fireplace in the mess hall—where Claudette and Barry once crooned about Michael rowing his boat ashore before their ill-fated shag in the barn—could do little to dispel the spirits of Camp Blood. Jump scare as Adrienne-Alice—retrofitted in yellow rain slicker and original cowboy boots—leapt out from behind the kitchen door, her first time back to camp, too. Then it was off to explore—nine locations in all—each locale loaded with filming facts and fan-pleasing trivia. The generator shed that had long ago gone dark made for pleasing photo ops with handfuls of arrows held strategically in place, while campers glimpsed the old barn locked up and safe. Then it was down to the lakeside we went, the lifeguard tower standing tall over the beach where Mrs. V lost her head. In Alice's cabin, the monopoly game was set up mid-play but there was no kitchen to be seen—that was all low-budget props and movie magic sheen. Use your imagination, too, to see where Marcie and Brenda brushed their teeth—sinks and toilet stalls were also temporary amenities for long-gone campers. Climbing upward, it's the archery range next. Nostalgia hits the bullseye and I'm sad thinking about Laurie's cancer and kids and how much crueler real-life can be than the movies. Back to the beach for picture playtime in the canoe with Adrienne-Alice and Mrs. V's rogue head and a machete prop, photographic brags for Facebook not likely to be topped. After dinner a surprise—a movie to be shown! It's lawn chairs and blankets and inflatable lakeside movie screen, Adrienne somewhere in the crowd feeling more surreal than any other camper ever or before. The feature rolls, the menacing syllabic score bouncing off the mountains and eerily echoing across the dusky lake. Tears amidst the murder—an odd thing indeed—with sentimental thoughts of buddy days with Dad and how he'd never believe I was in the thick of the movie now. End credits roll and campers scramble toward cars and exits, their return to camp over—but ours with more time on the meter. It's inaugural sleepover camp for the chosen ones who had the coin to pay for premium accommodations. I'm in Kevin's cabin—well, Brenda's, too—bottom bunk. I check under and above—no signs of stray arrows or hands, no dead Ned in sight. I hunker down in my sleeping bag—sounds dying down around the campsite—and strain my ears to listen for the cries of children in the night. Somewhere during the witching hour, I drifted off to sleep, dreams of final girls stepping out of movie screens like purple roses of Cairo supplementing my slumber. At five—still pitch dark—I have to pee worse than Marcie ever did, so I slide out of my sleeping bag and slip outdoors in search of the loo. Marcie got a fake stall, but I got a real plastic potty—even if mine didn't come with poetry on the walls. I step out into blackness to the sounds of crickets, shunning sleep to set off solo in search of a deeper communion with camp culture. The solitude of walking through Camp Crystal Lake, accompanied by only the crunch of gravel and a lone flashlight beam, is horror heaven. I retrace my footsteps from the day before, paying homage to the ghosts of this cinematic camp and memories of Saturday matinees with my Dad. I walk and walk and walk until I wander onto the beach where Alice ended her journey, too. Sitting peacefully, I watch the sun rise over the mountain, lightening the lake and bringing the camp into sharper focus. I gaze out at Alice's canoe in the distance and realize that I'm one happy camper.

Franchise Fatigue

Crazy Ralph warns them.
Summer-camp carnage begins.
Decapitation.

Back to summer camp.
Even the wheelchair guy dies.
What happened to Paul?

Cabin in the woods.
Terror in three dimensions.
Hockey-masked Jason.

The "final" chapter.
Jimmy finds the damn corkscrew.
Corey shaves his head.

A new beginning.
Tommy's halfway house horrors.
Ambulance guy kills.

Lightning bolts scare up
supernatural Jason.
Anchored in the lake.

Jason is freed by
telekinetic Tina.
Daddy saves the day.

Jason takes a trip
by charter boat to New York.
Big Apple showdown.

Voorhees blown to bits.
Eating Jason's putrid heart.
Joins Freddy in hell.

Jason goes to space.
Intergalactic slaughter.
Incineration.

Freddy meets Jason.
Two terror titans battle.
Freddy gives good head.

Franchise rebooted.
Return to Camp Crystal Lake.
Everyone yawns.

Les affections dangereuses

She was a California girl, with a French pretension and a Russian realism,
a breast-baring bisexual bohemian atheist and sometime Communist
who danced her way out of poverty.
Her mother sewed buttons in between piano lessons;
her father ran aground off the coast of Cornwall and drowned.

An occultist at a party once told her she had the gift of gesture
and indeed she favored fantasy over form,
despising the rigidity of convention and calling for the abortion of ballet
as her lissome form glided across worldwide stages
to the acclaim of those who appreciated improvisation.

She danced on banquet tables—garbed in tunics and togas—
at *grandes fêtes* recreating the *Bacchanalia* at Versailles
and posed for portraits that would capture her in immortal image.
Assignations with poets and playwrights dotted her
romantic résumé like bullet-pointed liaisons.

She booked passage on an ill-fated vessel, like her father once did,
dodging death like a lost *Final Destination* sequel.
But the grimmest of reapers took two of her illegitimate babes
in a runaway car that sunk in the Seine as well as the rebound baby
conceived in grief and sculpted of the finest Italian marble.

Death pursued her, and even moving to Moscow,
reciting sonnets with a trophy husband-poet eighteen years younger,
would not—could not—prevent the harbinger of heartbreak
that brought self-inflicted death from a hotel-room noose,
leaving the mother of the Isadorables alone in living death.

Grief stirred in her a voracious appetite for gigolo flesh
and impromptu drunken recitals in the public square.
Her offstage notoriety cast a shadow over the girl
who once danced her way out of poverty, now living off the benevolence of strangers
who still remembered the fluidity of her body rolls and compass turns.

The whisper of tryst with a French-Italian mechanic
would prove to be the last of life's critical entanglements,
as she hopped in the Bugatti convertible—long, hand-painted silk scarf
draped around her neck and flowing out behind her
as she drove out of sight proclaiming, "Farewell, my friends. I go to glory!"

Death—headstrong and persevering—tightened its grip
around her supple throat that mid-September night, crushing windpipe and wishes
as she soared through the air in one last moment of unexpected grace,
a pirouette for the ages as poor Isadora almost lost her head.
"Affectations can be dangerous," Gertrude Stein once said.

Grotesque Realities

We cringe, but we cannot look away.
The allure of the grotesque
appropriates attention and diverts brain cells
better spent elsewhere, on other things—
a fascination with the ghoulish and gross
rooted in reality and stitched into
the fabric of our everyday lives.

> In the traffic crawl that inches by,
> necks craned
> out of car windows lowered
> to repulse at the sight of auto-accident atrocity
> yet unable to tear eyes away
> from the roadside twist of metal
> entwined with bodies and blood.

> Scabs picked
> to see the wound beneath bleed afresh,
> unable to resist the deviant urge
> to scratch the itch or eat the chalk
> or even consume the couch cushions,
> their foam filling fluffy and satiating.
> Strange addictions indeed.

Reality-television—
purveyors of shock effect—
trailer park calamities and 600-pound lives,
boardwalk brawls at the Jersey shore
and hoarders buried deep in cat feces,
polygamous sister wives
and little people behaving badly.

Who doesn't like to recoil
when plastic surgery goes awry?
When all those Frankenstein monsters crafted
with Botox run through Beverly Hills?
What's better than a good squirm
when cysts are popped on backyard lawns
and pus falls like rancid cottage cheese?

Grotesqueries on parade
filing down avenues of madness
like misfit marching bands
and grand marshals of the Grand Guignol
riding on horror-show floats
festooned with skeletons and scarecrows—
both with vacant eyes blinded by bird boxes.

Night Terrors

Silence lay steadily
like opioid daydreams
integrated into the fabric of nightmares
that nocturnally regurgitate
months of psychoanalysis.

Subconscious stench intensifies
like malignant candle scents
wafting up from the rotted stomach linings
of dead cows knocked over and ripped apart
after standing too long in the fields.

Abstract hands caress gooseflesh
like aspirant serial killers,
stroke the fur-lined backs of small animals
before the crack of brittle necks
forecasts the homicidal inclinations to come.

Restlessness encroaches into slumber,
casting me into the throes of incubus dreams
in which all manner of bogeymen
grab and grope and gorge on spirit and skin
like demonic parasites that burrow in like ticks.

Malevolence infiltrates the reposing body,
extracting the toxic pus from the black veil of secrecy
that fuels these nighttime fears
like how maggots infest the necrotic tissue
of bad memories long repressed.

Sleep paralysis pushes down

with the strength of a strangler's grip,
disrupting the quietude of night
like the whistle of an angry hell-bound train
barreling down tracks coated with bone and blood.

Screams explode
like a nail-ridden bomb that detonates,
spraying private terrors and personal demons
in a cavalcade of nightmares and dreamscapes
that only daybreak can liberate me from.

Bury Your Revenge

You put me in a wooden box
and buried me six feet under,
my screams echoing off
planked prison walls
while my pounding fists
reverberate through
the packed black earth,
drawing worms and termites
that will eventually
find their way to my flesh.

I can feel the weight
of you standing above me;
I can picture your angry stance
and angrier eyes burrowing
through the soil between us
until the air is forced
from my deflating lungs,
as I sob apologies
through the knotted pine cover
of my new forever home .

In my heightened
sensory surroundings,
I think I can feel the vibrations
of your resentful tears
as they splatter the ground.
In the opaque silence,
I hear your voice, unrepentant
and unwavering in its conviction
that you had no other choice
but to bury your revenge.

Midnight at the Grindhouse

Marquee promises of deranged cinematic pleasures
flashed in boldly-lit lettering from above the seedy theater
where a boisterous soundtrack accompanied grainy images
of poorly edited scenes projected out into darkness within.

Velour seats soaked with the semen and the scent of cigarettes
from porn audiences past were bolted into concrete floors,
the underside of seats dotted with half-eaten Jujubes
and wads of masticated bubblegum.

Sticky armrests told tales of the kind not told to anyone
outside the circle of the grindhouse genteel—cinephiles
in search of a low-budget jewel and poverty tourists suckered
in for boobs and blood.

Irredeemable duds created by hacks on shoestring budgets
promised lurid content and tantalizing taboos on full display
for those who lacked a discriminating palate or a gag reflex—
from low-budget castrations to full-frontal flaccid fellatio.

Splices and snippets of sex and sadism cobbled together
in an unworthy narrative told tales of girls gone bad,
sentenced to prison where buxom Nazi matrons wielded kitten whips
and conducted cavity rummage sales with the snap of latex.

Biker chicks and whores on hot-rods vied for box office bucks
against the blood suckers of Blaxploitation and the hostile saltines
out to oppress, while Argento and Bertolucci cooked up
spaghetti westerns in the kitchen.

Nature ran amok—alligators, rabbits, and grizzlies, oh my!—

while death showed its many faces and thousands of maniacs
partook in bloody feasts while the hippies tripped and the
martial arts masters karate-chopped their way to notoriety.

The grindhouse had its heyday, but the show sold out some time ago.
Even the rats and roaches that once ran roughshod
over pavement cracks and moviegoers' toes vacated
long before the wrecking ball brought the demolition apocalypse.

But cinematic memory and nostalgia are not devils easily killed
with grindhouse grinding out a remarkably long shelf life
that repeats in matinees and midnight showings,
cults of congregants worshipping at its gritty feet.

Sitting in the reclining easy-chair pods of slick multiplex spaces,
gagging through trailers for saccharine rom-coms
and supercilious arthouse conceits choked with A-listers,
they long for the glory days of shlock.

No-frills degeneracy of a high-thrills retro sort
when the faceless ate the monkey's brains
and unrepentant rapists met the ends of chainsaw blades—
all in the comfort of low-rent accommodations and Jujube buffets.

Pagan Canticle

Voices raise
among the unconverted
in celebration of the moon-ritual
while hushed whispers
among paranoid peasants
speak of cautionary tales and talking-tos.

Sing-song incantations
among neo-pagan contemporaries—
witches, druids, goddess worshippers—
praise the sensual pleasures found
in Mother Earth's irreligious clitoris
that radiate out in hedonistic undulations.

Wiccan choruses intone
its Rede of consequentialist formulation,
"An' it harm none, do what ye will,"
while autonomous covens of thirteen
gather to create eclectic, syncretic paths
that deviate and dovetail without constraint.

Folk magicians rejoice
in the practical ceremonial magic
where the agnostic faithful assemble in
enchanted circles invoking custodians of cardinal points—
air, fire, water, and earth, united by aether—
and offer post-ritual gratitude to God-Goddess-Guardian.

The canticles of pagans
ring forth throughout the land
in salutation of the secular, in worship of the here and now.
Glorious voices sing of moments spent
exulting in the hedonism of the present
and the glorious rebuff of thankless asceticism.

Of Monsters and Men

A match
scraped alight
on the heel of a boot.

A brief flicker in the blackness.

A boy
scared, alone
hiding in a horse stall.

A small shadow in the corner.

Outside,
the rain falls
angrily, with purpose.

The wind cries out forlornly.

A man
—more monster—
lights the kerosene lamp.

The barn comes into focus.

Driven
to murder
when the weather turns bad.

A killer pluviophile.

"Come now,"
says the man,
"it's time to go, young man."

Silence ricochets back at him.

A horse
brays nearby
and the man is alert.

The corner-shadow shifts.

He walks
to the stall,
peering over the top.

Eye contact.

His face
not a face
but a horrible mask.

Of dead skin and teeth and bone.

Slowly,
he opens
the stall gate and steps in.

The boy cowers and cries out.

Nighttime
fever breaks,
releasing the boy.

Scary barnyard monster banished.

Monsters
without their
masks are just men in barns.

Who wait for small boys after all.

Sometimes
the horror of the worst fever dreams
is safer than reality.

Sometimes, it isn't.

My Ever-Changing Moods

As I break the surface
of my Ambien dreams,
my ever-changing moods
are as unpredictable
and fragile as pond ice
under the spell
of global warmth.

Yesterday, when I was mad,
mania felt like extra shots
of expresso in frothing lattes
served hot in controversial cups
that rile pious masses
and leave atheists
ostracized and without outrage.

Today, my mood is hopeful
like shelter dogs at opening bell—
tails wagging in anticipation
of the slightest kindness
or at least the kind of pity
bequeathed upon a deserted
discard with potential.

Tomorrow, my despair
will cast me deep
into Buffalo Bill's pit
leaving me little choice
but to snap fingernails
as I claw my way out.
Love your suit, Governor.

Moods flip like channels
on the TV remote—
and I can no longer discern
between hoarders and housewives,
dancing moms and strange addictions,
or bachelors behaving badly.
Will I ever get a rose?

Synapses fire on all cylinders
like malfunctioning spark plugs,
as disposition disintegrates
under the strain of stress
and the tyranny of obligation
that drowns me in hearspeak.
If not serenity now...

...how about a little later?

Eulogium for Nomadic Thoughts

My thoughts sometimes float off on daydreams
or untether from my parental hands
to wander through the park alone, those
nomadic notions that roam
like the Romani of lore and legend,
rootless, only taking sanctuary to regroup,
refuel, reform in a different configuration—
sometimes slipping out a back window, unseen.

I lament all the thoughts I've lost—
snippets of ideas that drift off on billowy puffs of clouds
that pass, unhurriedly, across my consciousness,
like misplaced keys or that agonizing search for a word
that hovers just out of range.
I stretch and strain and reach
with fingertips that fail to make contact.

Where do such vanished ideas go? These raw materials
for notions and postulations that go rogue
when the mind is distracted?
Is there a virtual depository in which they are dumped?
Perhaps they reside in great canvas bins,
like discarded Legos, haphazardly piled in
and waiting for the patient hands that will sift and sort,
block and build, until an impression forms, matures.

Perhaps such fleeting thoughts dissipate in the ether,
scattering snippets of potential that fail to hold together,
reentering the atmosphere and burning up
like spacecraft without heat shields.
Perhaps they swim like scallywag sperm

toward a cerebral uterus where they shimmy through
and plant a different seed altogether—or multiple
seeds that will grow a garden of ideas.

I like to believe that my nomadic meditations
are thought-orphans that find forever homes
traveling in great roving caravans,
picking up hitchhiking idea-vagrants
that huddle and gestate
before bursting from swollen thought-wombs
in a triumph of confluence.

Return to the Scene of the Crime

I've always liked the word *abscond*—
a word with character and gravitas
and literary sophistication
that's neither pretentious nor humble.
I almost wish it had an English "U"
because the English "U" classes up the joint,
don't you think?
Colours and flavours
and favourite neighbours.
Interesting, how a lone vowel
lends a sense of refinement
to the unrefined and unremarkable.
Tricky constructs,
those amalgamations of letters.
Uppercase and lowercase, like classism,
alive and thriving at Downton Abbey.
Care for a spot of tea, guvnor?
Tea time was a lovely notion, too,
with numbered lumps and flaky scones
and the warmth of a crackling fire
dispelling the gloom of misty moors
beyond arched window panes
admitting too much of the damp.
Cozy like a drawing room denouement
from a Christie novel about poisoned ladies
or murdered maids
or bludgeoned barons
where the red herrings
are consumed with clotted cream
and the clues laid out meticulously

like tarot cards ready
to foretell fortunes and calamities
with equal earnestness.
The butler always did it—
why were butlers so murderous?
Maybe they should unionize
for better wages and a health plan.
Maybe someone should add
Casual Friday to the week
so they could unbutton a bit,
get a little freaky.
Bowties too tight
make for cranky manservants.
No wonder they
clobber with candlesticks
in games of Clue brought to life.
Now there was a game
for the little grey cells
with colorful characters
as primary suspects
and an impressive arsenal
with ropes and revolvers,
daggers and spanners—
albeit with miniscule motives—
for their murderous gameplay,
traipsing from library to lounge,
kitchen to conservatory,
in homicidal hijinks.
The board game became a
madcap murder mystery movie
with the color of each character's car
matched perfectly to playing pieces.
Peacock was my favorite,
her hysterics very Lovey-like,
but it was hard to beat

the hot flaming flames that
erupted like a volcano
up the side of Madeline's face.
Geography dictated
movie's end—at least until
the home video release—
as one or another of the culprits
attempted to abscond.
Abscond.
I've always liked that word…

Scythes and Sickles

You betrayed me
with a kiss from your scythe,
sharp-bladed and sensually curved
as you shredded grass blades
in rhythmic whooshes.

I suppose it's possible
that you didn't see me there,
sprawled and sleeping
under the noonday sun
on that springtime day.

But surely, when I screamed,
shouted out in pain
as the crescent blade
lopped off a limb, surely,
then, you knew I was there.

Did you think the grass had hardened,
as you swung to and fro,
meeting resistance with every
mighty swing of your instrument
as it made its way through flesh and bone?

I wonder, as I lay bleeding,
how many other souls
you'd trodden over,
alternating between scythe and sickle
to carve them out of existence.

I deliberate if other men

working in the fields beside you
notice that you spend more time
in some grassy spots than others.
Do they admire your posturing perfectionism?

It seems disingenuous to me
to have been so gracelessly
mowed over by you,
denying my affections and advances
and taking a billhook to my heart.

You're a callous cropper,
one who ploughs roughshod
over everything in your path
with scant regard
for what you leave in wake.

Now I lie here—bits of me
here and there—
scattered amidst
the handsomely groomed
swathe of verdant grass.

If I close my eyes,
I can still hear the cadenced
whisper of your scythe
pressing forward for
wild parcels unknown.

You harvest what you sow.
You harvest what you sow.
You harvest what you sow…

Remnants

I.
Ghosts flutter
behind closed eyelids
like white sheets
left out on clotheslines
billowing on the wind.

Spectral visions
play out behind milky orbits,
coated with cataract sheen
but no less clear
in their ability to see.

Old memories
grow more distant in time
that passes too slowly
and too quickly with
clock-like imprecision.

II.
I am old and alone,
left with these remnant thoughts,
kept company by
all manner of ghosts
floating by on aberrant daydreams.

Why do they come—
these phantoms of long ago—
to taunt or terrorize?
As I sit unaccompanied in my years,

I fear I already know the answer.

The ghosts have come
to do the bidding of conscience,
ethereal purveyors of grim reckoning
that slither behind ocular cracks
to commandeer the projector.

III.
Images flicker
as blooper reels roll,
projecting my worst roles
onto walls gilded
with ancient wall coverings.

Tears fall
as sins come back anew,
reminding me of the discoloration
of my tarnished soul
now awash in contrition.

Penitent outbreaths
escape on despondent sighs
as I rise from my chair,
walking stick in hand,
ready to depart with the ghosts.

Stratagem

I want to harden.
I wish it, desire it—
to turn softness to stone,
to toughen like the calluses
on the hands of civilization.
I want to learn to live
without the consequences
of actions—hard, decisive, absolute.

     I want to harden.
     I covet it, crave it—
     to crush empathy like a hollow skull,
     to hammer compassion into subservience.
     I want to cast shadow
     on light corners
     in a darkening world.

          I want to harden.
          I want it, long for it it—
          to emanate apathy and indifference,
          to kill kindness with wanton heartlessness.
          I want to be a blight
          on what little goodness resides
          in the atrophying hearts of man.

               I want to harden.
               I need it, require it—
               to survive the launched offensive,
               to outmaneuver the antagonism.
               I want to outwit, outplay, outlast.
               I want to live to tell another lie.
               I want to be the last snowflake standing.

Ivan & The Terribles

Ivan advised
a suitable place to crash
as the pot-smoking punk quartet
buzzed down the country lane
in their pimped-out touring van
that took curves too fast
and the wrong shortcut
on the way home from a gig—
got caught up
in an agrarian steel claw
and hit the skids
as they rolled down an
embankment toward obscurity.

Cheers to the drummer
who first smelled something funny
as canister chloroform filled the van
and the band went six feet under
with burlap hoods and
vocal cords slit with precision kindness.
They reluctantly landed a new gig—
in a garden—being funnel-fed cattle feed
to make them plump enough
for sausage casings. After all,
it takes all kinds of critters
to make these kinds of fritters.

Spiral wheels spin
in psychedelic gyrations,
entrancing a captive audience
held tight in earthen grip

so necks don't suffer the snap—
it's harvest time at the farm,
prepping the piggies for market.
Stripped and strung
and washed with care,
meat is ripped from muscle
and bone and sliced into strips
to become savory smoked morsels.

Absence made hearts grow fonder
and fame—a fickle and funny thing indeed—
surged amongst the sentimental sympathies
of the music-loving masses.
Ivan and company rose
like a phoenix from the ashes,
number one with a bullet.
Ghosts to the concertgoers
who packed in tight in tribute
to the vanished band
as they nibbled beef jerky sticks,
terrible in their aftertaste.

The Actor

He hitchhiked his way to Hollywood
before afterschool specials that warned of such things,
barefoot in crop-topped tee and denim cutoffs,
thumb extended west. The rides were free
but the cost was steep in reclining bucket seats,
ticking off mile markers with his mouth.

His head was filled with movie-set daydreams—
the chaos of cameras and cranes being mounted and moved,
wardrobe racks rolling by, writers revising last-minute lines,
actors arriving on set to the appreciative clap of the crew,
hair coiffed and make-up applied, maybe a cram at craft services—
before the clapboard clacks and the director yells "Action!"

At his very first audition, he heard suggestive whispers
about Hunter and Hudson, Coward and Clift,
and a gilded age of golden showers as he deposited headshots
and took to the casting couch like a hungry babe to the breast,
memorizing lines on his back while movie moguls filled him
with empty promises of his name in lights above the marquee.

II.
The curtain rises and the audience gasps,
his beauty disorienting, almost painful to behold—
chiseled cheekbones with a jawline for days, pouty lips and carved physique—
he captures hearts and stirs loins of all persuasions and designs.
The part has few lines and even fewer wardrobe requirements
but still earns him standing ovations of thunderous applause.

He receives admirers with doe-eyed innocence,

eccentric socialites and flamboyant financiers and cultivated art collectors—
all members of café society glitterati who want to luxuriate in his presence
in a shared dressing room with cinderblock walls.
He accepts them all, taking in their words of approbation
while letting them siphon off specks of his beauty like psychic vampires.

He never truly realizes that he's but one of the boys in this band,
a bit player in John Wayne garb hustling his way into a birthday party,
the gift that keeps on giving after hours at after parties
since there wasn't a pair of pants that didn't hang perfectly
or a shirt that looked as comfortably snug on an Adonis body
that looked like it was sculpted from Ivory soap.

III.
Success was an elusive suggestion,
although he did dive bomb for Nazis in a flying circus for Corman
before an arthouse pilgrimage where he exorcised his demons
by dropping food at the buffet.
He was a character actor with no character,
a milquetoast understudy but never the lead.

The public reality of his playacting pretense
would become the bondage of pigeonholed constraint,
with limited cabaret engagements and Blueboy centerfolds
fleshing out his curriculum vitae
before he became a private dancer who kept his mind on the money
and his eyes on the wall of the bathroom stall.

The curtains close and the spotlight falls
as the actor takes his final bow amidst the deafening silence
of an empty theater long-ago left in the glow
of a solitary incandescent bulb trapped in a wire cage—
center stage—to guide the ghosts of failed careers
who mournfully long for the once great reception of their audience.

The Woods Are Dark

I fear these woods where feral fairies lurk,
My fellow thespians swallowed by fog,
Lost in forests of miasma and murk,
Among the night creatures of the black bog:

Quagmire that threatens every step,
Tricky as the machinations of sprites,
Who hoodwink rude mechanicals in prep,
For wedding theatrics festooned with frights:

Comedy quickly turns toward the tragic,
As death comes to this oft haunted marshland,
And woodland terrors turn sarcophagic,
Screams heard 'til grimaced mouths fill with quicksand:

Is this a curtain call as it would seem,
Or perchance a nightmare within a dream?

Horrors of the Female Persuasion

She's the little girl who lives down the lane
and the high school girl who's afraid to nap;
the suburban babysitter who carves a mean jack-o-lantern;
the bouncy camp counselor who fixes the cabin gutters;
the Sigma Phi sister who takes a terrifying train ride;
the addlepated prairie gal who throws a birthday bash.

She's the mother who owns the motel and dotes on her son
and the dearest movie-star mommy who hates wire hangers;
the auntie who stands in surrogate for her nephew in Oedipal rage;
the sister who helps her brother harvest critter-fritters;
the one who boogies with an axe-wielding brother at prom;
the baby-voiced sibling who steals the spotlight from her housebound sister.

She's the sorority sister with no place to go at Christmas
and the college coed taking night-school classes to get ahead;
the recent graduate who hates her headmistress;
the summer camp cook who fancies working with ~~kids~~ children;
the aspiring actress who auditions and ice skates;
the struggling stand-up with killer instincts desperate to land the part.

She's the good girl who loses her way in the funhouse
and the party planner who loses her heart in the laundromat;
the Quaalude poppin' Brit in flapper garb and garters who loses her head in the bed;
the accidental tourist who suffocates in a trap;
the bride-to-be who gets more than pre-wedding jitters;
the Warrant Officer who awakes from stasis to battle an acid-tongued alien adversary.

She's the midnight swimmer who bangs into buoys
and the fan-girl first reader who believes that misery loves company;
the raspy-voiced theater diva who receives the unwelcome attention of a fanboy;

the feminist newscaster who undergoes some hospital horrors;

the night-shift nurse who fellatiates fingers and dips in the hot tub;

the gerontologist who kisses a girl and develops a taste for blood and the good life.

She's the beauty with animal magnetism who attracts the attention of a king

and the bathing-suit bombshell who goes synchronized swimming in a black lagoon;

the fashionably-coiffed socialite who sidesteps seagulls in phone booths;

the secretary who showers to rinse the residue of dirty money;

the first-time mother with a Tannis root charm and a devilish delivery;

the crab-walking teen with a sour stomach and spinning head.

She's the bullied adolescent with menstrual cramps who unleashes telekinetic fury

and the videographer chasing witches in dark woods;

the girl-group spelunker who's terrified of tight spaces;

the popular Texas gal named Mandy whom all the boys love;

the graduate student beckoning sons of slaves with mirrored repetition;

the radio DJ who warns of things that go bump in the fog.

She's the jilted lover who boils bunnies

and the puppy-killing roomie who misses her stillborn twin;

the black widow who mates, kills, and turns tables;

the leg-crossing bisexual with an affinity for ice picks;

the imposter nanny who sets greenhouse traps that trigger asthma attacks;

the jazz-loving radio listener who likes to quote Poe.

She's the girl whose calls are coming from inside the house

and the one who takes a wrong turn;

the harried widow-mom who reads pop-up storybooks;

the one who thinks post-apocalyptic silence is golden;

the virgin who's desperate to break her hymen;

the one stalked by invisible sexual transmission.

She's the thoughtful girl who dwells on last summer's mistake

and the vengeful one who spits on graves;

the clever one who solves puzzle boxes and summons Cenobites;

the little one calling out from television static;

the zealous one preaching biblical wrath from grocery store aisles;
the accidental feminist whose vagina has quite the snap.

She's both predator and prey—a coat of many colors—
a damsel in distress and a fierce femme fatale;
a scene-stealing sidekick who elicits an empathy response,
and a formidable final girl with an axe to grind;
a pop culture icon who chainsaws her way into our hearts,
an unlikely academic discipline and subject for thought.
Hear her roar and listen to her scream and watch her kill and see her survive.
She's a woman in horror: Cheer her. Fear her. Reengineer her. Revere her.

Signs of Life

You lie there, hooked
to the life support machine.
Tubes of varying lengths and girths
enter and exit your body
like freeway off-ramps.

To the world, outside
of yourself, you appear
peaceful, serene—like
the reposing lead
in a timeless fairytale.

A soft kiss does not awaken
you from fairytale slumber
and instead you sleep,
ceaselessly, with no respite
from your internal nightfall.

Sometimes I wonder—watching
your chest rise and fall
in mechanically-induced repetition—
if you really are awake,
trapped on the inside, looking out.

Entombed inside yourself, aware
of everything around you—
faces, words, grim prognoses—
you eavesdrop by default,
overhearing gossip and innuendo.

You hear things, astonished
and appalled, a silent witness
to the sex, lies, and videotape
playing out in the flesh
like a bedbound voyeur.

You lie there, listening
to deathbed confessions and
apologies and admonishments
for leaving too soon
even though you are right here.

You scream aloud, inside
the prison of your mind,
banging on the walls
of your unconsciousness
that imprison you.

Behind your eyes, pleading
for someone to hear you,
you will a lid to twitch,
a tear to drop, an eye
to burst forth from its socket.

You are entombed, alive
within an ossuary of flesh
and blood that pumps through veins,
left screaming endlessly
within an unending echo chamber.

You lie there, hooked
to the life support machine.
I stand sentinel, hyper-sensitive
to the slightest tremble, watching
for any signs of life within.

Maternity Ward

I placed a picture of you in a frame today.

It was an odd thing to do, considering…

I've tried to view you through an emotional gauze that blurs the blunt edges of memory—
it's just what I do. It's what I must do, to cope and avoid and circumvent memories
like ducking adolescent onslaught in gym class dodgeball games.

As I trimmed around your pretty face—clipped from an old wedding photo
long salvaged from the discards of divorce—to set you in the circular slot,
I tried to remember you in any way but the way I'm condemned to.
If I try hard enough, I see snippets of images: you, happy—light and full,
illuminating rooms with an exquisite smile and your sweet, lilting voice.

There was a kindness in you, too—fleeting as it was. I remember it, but it struggled so
against the darkness within, the one with no name.
Like storm clouds, your dark passenger would cast shadow across your beautiful face.
With sudden onset, its duration could be marked by hours, sometimes days.

I can see you stretched out on the couch—that Victorian knockoff with the ornate flowers—
flipping through ladies' magazines and chain-smoking Benson & Hedges in your nightgown.
How I hated that couch—positioned dead center in the house—forever blocking my
escape from the hallway leading out from my childhood bedroom.

A simple trip to the kitchen for a snack was like a religious pilgrimage—full of prayers
and promises to the baby Jesus if he'd just let me get past you unscathed.

Sometimes, if I was lucky, I slipped by while your eyes were fixated on the latest *Cosmo* quiz
or too disinterested in your own life to care what I did. Hallelujah moments when I snuck
out the front door, grateful for interim release from the toxic suffocation
and already forgetting my promises to baby J.

Other times, providence was not mine to behold.
You'd be between pages or staring off into space,
catching even my faintest exhale in your peripheral vision.

As I finagle your picture into the frame now, the gauze grows mercifully thicker
and I block the images.

Why the picture now? I do not know.
It's been many years since you left—a few more since you left that final time
without so much as a nod in my direction.
You were consistent, I'll grant you that, without an ounce of prejudice.
Points for your maternal aggression right up until the buzzer.

Death made your vanishing act complete.
I'll admit—in this weak moment, looking at your sepia-tinged image—
that you crept up on me when the death certificate arrived,
sucker-punched me with unpredicted force I did not foresee.
You, this woman I knew intimately yet not at all.

Oddments of information—address, occupation, next of kin, cause of death—
are the paltry scraps you left me to piece together, three decades of gaps.
Why do I want to know, you ask? I do. I don't.
Call it morbid curiosity. Call it detached interest.
Call it whatever the fuck you want.

I may be tasked with existing in this earthly vessel,
but I long ago rejected drowning in your sea of lies and pretense.
Indifferent details on a typewritten piece of paper
protect me from that so I indulge my prurience.
Was it sudden? A lingering affliction? Did you suffer? Do I care?

Grief is not static. It changes as we change, and I accept that.
My grief for you exists in a purgatory of contradictory emotions,
and I willingly allow it wallow there.

It is without urgency.

You are reduced to apparition now, a ghost in a circular frame—
and I, a ward of your maternal specter,
will be haunted by daydreams and nightmares alike.

For Theresa Rose Danko (1945-2015)

You and I and Us

Our story began
with a question
and ended
with a body count.

All you had to say
was no—
not your maybe
that opened doors
to perceived chance.

I tried to warn you
with shifty eyes
and a perspired brow,
that disconcerting twitch
in my left hand—
the one that held the axe.

You acquiesced
to dinner and a kiss,
accepting the bouquet
of corner-store carnations
with demure charm
and a decree of delight
even as you sneezed.

I wish you hadn't feigned
interest in my story—
most of which was fabricated

to hide my mediocrity—
or shared details of your own
that bespoke an
intimacy of intention
you never meant to keep.

You made a choice
not to cut ties
even after the first
telltale signs
of a glitch in the machine
or those photos of you
on my laptop long before
that first *random* encounter
that brought us here.

You asked
all the right questions
even though
you already knew
the answers
to the how's and why's,
even though you
suspected there was
more you didn't
want to know.

I should have come clean
right then and there,
but I knew that even
wiped slates leave residue
of the past like snails
leave trails of slime.
I tried to reason away
my madness as mere folly,
but you were smart enough—

and foolish enough—
not to play along.

You shouldn't have been
so sharing with others,
leaving details—our details—
to us, for us to process
and deliberate. Instead,
you put us under a microscope
for others—outsider others—
to poke and prod in
hypothesis of what
you already knew.
Why did you play coy?
For validation or vindication?

I was responsible for what I did;
you were responsible for me
doing what I did.
You led me on, led me to it
like the horse to water
and I drank, drank *thirstily*.
It wasn't as hard
as I'd imagined it to be,
no more than for the exterminator
tasked with eliminating
uninvited vermin.
Now, we can talk—clear the air.
It's just you and I and us.

Final Breath, Drawn

His final breath
draws in uncertainty.

What if the atheism
his mind held fast and dear
was the wrong construct after all?
Maybe doubt was the better course.

Does plausible denial
warrant forgiveness
from this willful disbelief?

Or are the faithless
cast downward on torrents
of flaming meteorites
and rainfalls of molten lava?

Fire and brimstone—
it might be true.
So might red devils
with pitchforks and forked tongues.

He worries that his final breath
may not release him
from the unbearable pain after all,
that this earthly suffering
might endure, be eternal.
What then?

What if there is a hereafter—
like the duality of spectrum ends
promised in catechism classes—
and his pragmatic choice was not
the lesser of two evils?

Vince A. Liaguno

What if the road to hell
isn't paved with all those
good intentions after all but instead
rutted with denials and denunciations
of such an epilogue?

Breath draws in tighter
until the room is filled to capacity.
He holds it in fear
of miscalculation.
For how long, he knows not.
Only that he must hold it
if there is indeed to be an eternity—
it's inconvenient to him
on this death bed, in these bedclothes.

He will not go gently
into the sweet good night
a mistaken man.
Even in the harsh throes
of death's firm grip,
there is the matter of pride.

His eyes widen now,
bulging in the terror of possibility,
as the tectonic plates of his certitude
shift beneath him.

His final breath,
drawn in so tight,
for so long, releases—
exhaling him
into the interminably
darkest of nights.

There—in the obscurity
of this no place with no direction—
he hears *something*…
but there is no more breath
from which to draw.

Afterword

I am an unapologetic pop culture junkie. Movies, television, books, and music have informed every nook and cranny of my life. It's no surprise then that the collection of poetry you hold in your hands is riddled with references to such. Whether it's a borrowed song title—as in the case of "Monday Shutdown" or "My Ever-Changing Moods" (thanks Martha Davis and The Motels and The Style Council, respectively)—or a nod to an author colleague (yes, there's one for each of you, Josh Malerman and Stephen Graham Jones), I've liberally sprinkled in pop culture references throughout. Of course, there's an entire poem in tribute to the career of the preeminent scream queen of my generation—the incomparable Jamie Lee Curtis.

But since my heart belongs to horror, this collection is generously peppered with horror (and a few non-horror) movie references. So many, in fact, that Stephanie Wytovich, my trusted adviser on this project, suggested that I create a list of them. And who am I to shrug off a brilliant idea?

Movie Reference by Poem

"Monday Shutdown"
Godzilla (1954)
The Fog (1980)
Halloween (1978)
Friday the 13th (1980)
A Nightmare on Elm Street (1984)

"Frankenstein's Grammar"
Frankenstein (1931)

"Tyro"
The Silence of the Lambs (1991)

"Demo Reel"
Halloween (1978)
The Fog (1980)
Prom Night (1980)

Terror Train (1980)
Road Games (1981)
Halloween II (1981)
Halloween: H2O (1998)
Virus (1999)
Halloween: Resurrection (2002)
Halloween (2018)

"Lost Traveler"
The Fog (1980)

"Other"
The Day the Earth Stood Still (1951)

"Carnivàle"
The Funhouse (1981)
Death Becomes Her (1992)
Godzilla (1931)

"Random Selection"
Sophie's Choice (1982)

"The Night He Came Out"
Halloween (1978)

"American Psychos"
American Psycho (2000)

The House That Jack Built (2018)

Maniac (1980)

Copycat (1995)

Mr. Brooks (2007)

Se7en (1995)

Psycho (1960)

The Talented Mr. Ripley (1999)

The Hitcher (1986)

Kiss the Girls (1997)

Saw (2004)

Henry: Portrait of a Serial Killer (1986)

The Bone Collector (1999)

"Summer Camp, Parts I and II"
Friday the 13th (1980)

"Franchise Fatigue"
Friday the 13th (1980)

Friday the 13th Part 2 (1981)

Friday the 13th Part III (1982)

Friday the 13th: The Final Chapter (1984)

Friday the 13th: A New Beginning (1985)

Friday the 13th Part VI: Jason Lives (1986)

Friday the 13th Part VII: The New Blood (1988)

Friday the 13th Part VIII: Jason Takes Manhattan (1989)

Jason Goes to Hell: The Final Friday (1993)

Jason X (2001)

Freddy vs. Jason (2003)

Friday the 13th (2009)

"Les affections dangereuses"
Final Destination (2000)

"My Ever-Changing Moods"
The Silence of the Lambs (1991)

"Return to the Scene of the Crime"
Downton Abbey (2010-2015)

Clue (1985)

"Ivan & The Terribles"
Motel Hell (1980)

"Horrors of the Female Persuasion"
The Little Girl Who Lives Down the Lane (1976)

A Nightmare on Elm Street (1984)

Halloween (1978)

Friday the 13th (1980)

Terror Train (1980)

Happy Birthday to Me (1981)

Psycho (1960)

Mommie Dearest (1981)

Butcher, Baker, Nightmare Maker (1981)

Motel Hell (1980)

Prom Night (1980)

Whatever Happened to Baby Jane? (1962)

Black Christmas (1974)

Night School (1981)

The House of Sorority Row (1982)

Friday the 13th (1980)

Curtains (1983)

Curtains (1983)

The Funhouse (1981)

My Bloody Valentine (1981)

Hell Night (1981)

Tourist Trap (1979)

He Knows You're Alone (1980)

Alien (1979)

Jaws (1976)

Misery (1990)

The Fan (1981)

Visiting Hours (1982)

Halloween II (1981)

The Hunger (1983)

King Kong (1933)

Creature From the Black Lagoon (1954)

The Birds (1963)

Psycho (1960)

Rosemary's Baby (1968)

The Exorcist (1973)

Carrie (1976)

The Blair Witch Project (1999)

The Descent (2006)

All the Boys Love Mandy Lane (2013)

Candyman (1992)

The Fog (1980)

Fatal Attraction (1987)

Single White Female (1992)

Black Widow (1987)

Basic Instinct (1992)

The Hand That Rocks the Cradle (1992)

Play Misty for Me (1971)

When a Stranger Calls (1979)

Wrong Turn (2003)

The Babadook (2014)

A Quiet Place (2018)

Cherry Falls (2000)

It Follows (2015)

I Know What You Did Last Summer (1997)

I Spit on Your Grave (1978)

Hellraiser (1987)

Poltergeist (1982)

The Mist (2007)

Teeth (2007)

Acknowledgements

As much as writing is a solitary act committed in private, it's also a group effort when you pull the camera back and expand the angle to consider influences, beta readers, and those involved with getting the finished work into the readers' hands. To that end, I'd like to thank Lisa Morton, Chad Helder, and Marge Simon for their early feedback and encouragement. Their generous and unbridled enthusiasm for this project has been a gift that spurred me toward the finish line. Heartfelt thanks to Stephanie Wytovich, a true dark poet of extraordinary talent and wisdom, whose exhaustive, line-by-line critique of these poems brought this collection into sharper focus.

I'd like to thank Rich Ristow who afforded a fledgling poet patience and the benefit of his keen editorial eye almost a decade ago. Both "Chatroom Hustler" and "Tyro" are better poems for it. Likewise, I'd like to thank the other editors who have given a home to my poetry over the years: Peter Giglio, Angela Yuriko Smith, Eugene Johnson, Stephanie M. Wytovich, and James Aquilone.

Thanks (and my enduring love) to my partner in life, Brian Scott Charles, for encouraging our move to Michigan, which first sparked my interest in writing this collection. In that same vein, I'd like to thank all the wonderful Michiganders who befriended a skeptical New Yorker and made me feel welcome in their beautiful state—even if they're entirely too cheerful at checkout counters and drive-thru windows. Bless their hearts.

And, as always, thanks to my beloved father, Vincent Liaguno, who supported my love of scary movies and never once complained while sitting through horror film after horror film on Saturday afternoons. I'm sure there were probably a hundred different things he would have rather been doing—anything, really, than watching Jamie Lee Curtis run, screaming, from yet another masked killer with a butcher knife/axe—but, if he did, he never let on. I hope with his final breath drawn, he received all the love and light of the universe. I miss you, Dad.

About the Author

Vince A. Liaguno is an award-winning writer, anthologist, critic, and poet. He is the Bram Stoker Award®-winning editor of *Unspeakable Horror: From the Shadows of the Closet* (co-edited with Chad Helder) and the acclaimed *Other Terrors: An Inclusive Anthology* (co-edited with Rena Mason), which was a finalist for both the prestigious Shirley Jackson and World Fantasy Awards. His debut novel, 2006's *The Literary Six*, was a tribute to the slasher films of the eighties and won an Independent Publisher Award (IPPY).

Healthcare administrator by day, pop culture enthusiast by night, his jam: books, slasher films, and Jamie Lee Curtis. He is a member (and former secretary) of the Horror Writers Association (HWA), International Thriller Writers (ITW), and the National Book Critics Circle (NBCC). Vince currently resides in the mitten-shaped state of Michigan.